Date Due

The Indians of Northeastern America

L.F. BJORKLUND

THE INDIANS
OF NORTHEASTERN
AMERICA

Karna L. Bjorklund

Illustrated by Lorence F. Bjorklund

DODD, MEAD & COMPANY · NEW YORK

Frontispiece: Chippewa warrior

3/30/70
4.95

970.4
B556i

To my mother and father, whose interest, guidance, and encouragement made possible the writing of this book

Contents

The Indians of Northeastern America

Chapter 1

------------------◆◆------------------

THE FIRST AMERICANS

IT WAS OVER a thousand years ago on a northern island shore that a man with painted skin stood watching the sea. He stared in disbelief and then fled in terror. For into his world the sea was bringing a magnificent "canoe," unlike any other he had ever seen. But even more than that, the strange vessel was bringing men—men of light skin with fair hair and blue eyes.

The white man had reached the continent of North America and the Indian would never again be the sole inhabitant of this land.

The year was 1000 A.D. when the Viking, Leif Ericson, sailed from Greenland in his dragon-prowed long-ship with its striped square sail. In this undecked vessel the courageous Norse sea rovers had crossed the stormy North Atlantic to settle in Iceland; then later in Greenland. From there Leif sailed to the island of Newfoundland. He called the land Vinland and established a settlement, the remains of which exist today at L'Anse au Meadow in northern Newfoundland. This was the island of the Eskimo and the Beothuk Indian.

According to Norse sagas, Thorvald, the brother of Leif Ericson, was the first white man to meet a native American, known to the Vikings as a "skraeling." Thorvald was killed by the natives with an arrow, a sad prelude to the fate of the Norse colony in Vinland, which was soon abandoned. The Greenland settlement persisted for five hundred years before it too vanished.

Yet the Europeans had in fact met the "Americans" and this was but the first of these encounters. The next white man to meet a native of North America would do so almost five hundred years after Leif the Lucky ventured to Newfoundland, and to him would be ascribed the credit for discovery of this land.

Christopher Columbus landed on San Salvador in 1492 and, believing himself to be in India, promptly called the brown-skinned natives he found there, Indians, a misnomer which has persisted throughout the centuries.

Many adventurers would sail westward across the Atlantic in the years following that first landing of Columbus and some would never return to tell of their exploits. Among those who are known to have explored the coasts of North America was the Venetian, John Cabot, who in his little vessel, the *Matthew*, skirted the fringes of what is now eastern Canada. Putting ashore in the ship's longboat, he set foot on what he believed to be the land of the Khan. To John Cabot it seemed strange that the appearance of the land did not compare with the reports of numerous Asian travelers which he had studied.

Several years later, a Portuguese nobleman, Gaspar Corte-Real, in his search for a route to Asia, may have landed where Cabot had been, for he found an Indian wearing Venetian earrings. He believed he had landed in Asia on the heels of another European trading vessel.

It had become apparent by the early sixteenth century that it was not Asia but, in truth, a New World which had been discovered by these westward expeditions. Now it was the quest of countless voyagers and adventurers to find a passage by which ships could reach the East and thereby breach this terrestrial obstruction. In search of this fabled corridor came Verrazano, Cartier, Frobisher, Davis, Baffin, and Hudson. Intriguing accounts of their exploits kindled in the minds of Europeans an irresistible urge to benefit from the fabulous new land. The lust for gold, the dream of glory, and freedom to worship were primary encouragements to embark upon this venture.

So to the primeval homelands of the Algonkians and the Iroquois came the English, the Dutch, the French, and the Swedes with their trading companies, soldiers, adventurers, colonists, and pilgrims. To the newcomers, the Indian imparted his ancient knowledge of how to survive in the woodlands of the great Northeast, but what the Indian received in return cost him his home, his liberty, and his very life.

The first Americans were not the Europeans who voyaged from the east nor were they the woodland natives whom the white man met. The first Americans had made a prehistoric arrival into the New World from that very western land to which the earliest explorers had hoped to sail.

In an age now obscured by the passing of more than a hundred centuries, a small band of homeless fur-clad hunters rested at the tidemarks of an Arctic sea that ebbed on the eastern coast of the continent now called Asia. The wild game they followed did not pause but continued eastward over a narrow isthmus and, after a time, the hunters again took up the chase. Night descended swiftly and the hunters slept while the cold fire of the northern lights glittered above the frozen wastes. The frigid dawn found them already in pursuit of the huge deer and bison straying across this barren stretch in a constant search for grazing land. As the last rays of the sun signaled another halt in their trek, the weary travelers looked out over a lowland which broadened to the north and south. Soon the game they hunted would come upon a grassy valley and here both animals and men could cease their journeys for a time.

Unwittingly, these Stone Age nomads had set foot upon the mainland of the North American continent, the first of mankind

Crossing the land bridge

to come upon the Western Hemisphere by a land route.

Countless generations and thousands of years would pass before descendants of these earliest Americans would cross the river later called the Mississippi into northeastern America and become the Algonkian and Iroquoian Indians of that region.

These Paleolithic people lived a simple life in which food was their greatest necessity. They had no knowledge of civilization, few skills, and only stones with which to fashion their tools and weapons. They had no thought of exploring, pioneering, or colonizing, and a bridge of land meant little other than that it might lead to another day's meal. Small bands of hungry people, several families perhaps, settling in a new valley, lived as their ancesters had for centuries. When food became scarce or their population too large, a few members of the group moved on, over the next ridge or beyond the nearby mountains.

Following his primitive day-to-day struggle for existence, the Stone Age man had wandered slowly across the face of Asia eastward onto the tip of Siberia. His pattern did not alter when the strip of land linking Siberia to Alaska was crossed. The peopling of North America was unhurried, occurring over thousands of years, beginning some twenty, thirty, or more thousands of years ago. At that time no one was aware of a migration, and the discovery of a new continent did not occur to these people for whom the arduous business of living occupied every thought. These first settlers did not remember a starting point and likewise their descendants, who came to be called Indians, had no recollection of their true origin.

The Indians do, however, have many stories by which they explain their existence. The Chippewas tell this story of the first Indians.

The Great Manitou, a ruling spirit of this Algonkian tribe, once took the form of a giant bird which lived among the pipestone rocks in the Land of Peace. Clutching in his talons the wild buffalo which he snatched from the prairies below, the great bird flew to his nest where his frequent feasts forever stained the rocks a bloody red. The Great Serpent, also older than mankind, found the nest of the fearsome bird while it was away. There was one egg in the nest, which moved when the Serpent came near. The Manitou heard the egg moving and swooped down upon

15

The Great Manitou

the treacherous snake with a huge rock in its claws. He killed the Great Serpent but also broke open the egg, whereupon a full-grown man rose out of the broken shards. The man was unable to move, for the great rock remained on his feet, pinning him to the rocky ledge. The Manitou would not free his captive until he had taught him many things.

The man learned how to make a bow and arrow and how to hunt the buffalo and use its hide for clothing and its meat for food. He learned the language of the birds and many other useful things. This first man was slow to learn and stood for a long time among the pipestone rocks before the Manitou was finally satisfied with his achievements. One morning when the man awoke, he found a woman standing beside him. The Manitou then removed the stone from the man's feet and the first two people ran to the prairie. They were Indians and all of mankind knows that they were the first to live on the earth.

One version of a modern Iroquois creation legend explains the origin of those tribes in this way. Long ago people lived beyond the sky because deep waters covered the entire earth. Soaring birds filled the air and great monsters inhabited the waters. In the land of the Sky People the chief's daughter became very ill and no cure could be found. A wise man told the people that they had to dig up a tree and place the ailing girl beside the open hole. As the people were digging, the tree suddenly fell through the hole carrying with it the chief's lovely daughter. The tree plummeted downward to the great water where two huge swans were swimming. The swans heard a clap of thunder and, looking up, they saw the young girl falling from the sky.

While the tree sank to the bottom of the sea, the swans caught the girl and supported her upon their overlapping wings, protecting her from the terrors of the water. They carried her to the Great Turtle, Master of all the Animals, who volunteered his strong back as a plinth upon which to set the maiden. First, however, he ordered that the animals swim to the spot where the tree had sunk and dive down for some of the earth which clung to its roots. When this magic earth had been recovered and placed upon his back, the Great Turtle began to grow into a large island. As the world increased in size, quakings of the earth were felt by the woman as the monster beneath her stretched and moved. Eventually, two sons were born to her, one who made the maize, fruit, tobacco, and all good things that grow, and the other who created weeds, vermin, and other evils upon the earth.

After many ages the Sky Holder, a powerful Iroquois god, created a special race surpassing all others in beauty, strength, and bravery. From inside the island he brought forth six pairs destined to become the greatest of all people. These six pairs became the Mohawks, Onondagas, Oneidas, Cayugas, Senecas, and Tuscaroras, the six tribes of the famous Iroquois League.

As with most people seeking to satisfy questions about their own earliest beginnings, the Indian developed such stories to help explain the things which he did not understand. Living closely with nature as he did, the Indian's stories naturally included the animals with which he was familiar and, in many cases, animals are people or become people. It is also characteristic of most origin stories that the people involved consider themselves to be the first men on earth or to be special in some way. This is seen in both the Chippewa and Iroquois creation legends, and the Indian may be closer to the truth than he realizes.

The date for man's entry into the New World is almost as vague as that for man's origin itself. It is quite certain that man did not originate on this continent because, up to now, no evidence of Neanderthal or other pre-Stone Age man has been found in North or South America. All remains found on both continents are of the modern species, *Homo sapiens,* which means that man must have come to this part of the world from somewhere else. The oldest human fossil so far discovered in North America, for which the date is considered accurate, is a woman's skeleton 12,000 years old, found in Texas in 1953, indicating that humans have inhabited this continent at least that long. Several sites throughout the western part of the United States have yielded charcoal from the fires of primitive man and samples of burned mammoth bones which, when tested, were found to be at least 20,000 to 30,000 years old. Wood from one of early man's campsites at Lewisville, Texas, is thought to be as much as 37,000 years old. On the basis of such findings, many authorities claim human occupation of North America as long ago as 30,000 years, while others suggest that even 70,000 years is not an unlikely date. The use of radiocarbon analysis and the more recent magnetic dating method may soon push the date of man's first appearance in the New World even farther back into pre-history.

From established evidence there seems to be no doubt that early man made his intercontinental trip before the last glacier retreated 10,000 years ago, but how long before or how many times the trip was made awaits further disclosures. Archaeologists have yet to find any evidence left behind by America's true discoverers, if indeed they left any at all, as they passed through that remote northern wilderness now called Alaska.

Scientists believe that the early migrants from Asia, known as Paleo-Indians, came in waves. The very first primitive men to traverse the ancient land bridge to America belonged to a long-headed race which made the crossing into the New World before the development and spread of the Mongoloid people into northeastern Asia. These people brought with them only stone or bone implements and, probably, the use of fire. Successive waves—and their number is unknown—were of a round-headed, Mongoloid type, more advanced in many ways over their predecessors. These later groups had profited by contacts with

An early Indian

other early Asian people and were more inventive and adaptive, bringing with them better tools, greater skills, and the domesticated dog. Some may have even had the technology to make skin boats in which they might have crossed the dark, icy waters between the continents when a land link no longer existed.

Geology helps support the theory that there was once a land bridge across the Bering Sea. Throughout the past 500,000 years the earth experienced the comings and goings of tremendous glaciers in a period known as the Great Ice Age. Within this time four gigantic ice sheets reached into the heart of North America, only to recede again with the passage of time. In the formation of glaciers, great amounts of water are transformed into ice, lowering the level of the sea and exposing portions of the ocean bottom. During one or more of these times the Bering Strait was dry land and the Diomede Islands, emerging now as stepping stones across the channel, were then high mountains looming above a frozen tundra or perhaps a grassy plain. Across this isthmus lumbered the huge woolly mammoth, recording its ancient trail for the paleontologist by its large tusks which are unearthed today as fossils in Alaskan soil. Great deer, giant ground sloths, and bison made their way into North America and, in turn, the Paleo-Indian could well have followed that ridge of land onto the threshold of this continent.

These earliest men journeyed between 10,000 foot-thick glaciers as they made their way from the Alaskan plain southward through the ice-free Mackenzie Valley. Other unglaciated corridors existed from time to time, which may have led successive bands of human migrants to the warmer climates. Among them, a hundred mile-wide passage cut through Alberta to the plains of Saskatchewan, and similar routes followed the Yukon, Peace, or Liard River valleys. Much later arrivals may even have come by way of the Aleutian Islands.

Eventually, the glaciers began to recede and as millions of square miles of ice slowly melted, vast quantities of water were unleashed and returned to the oceans, raising the sea level, covering the coastal lowlands, and obliterating any traces man might have left of his crossings. As the land bridge sank beneath the Arctic seas, North America was again severed from Asia. Few, if any, brave adventurers would seek this continent again for 9,000 years, and the pre-historic Indian was left alone to rule the Americas.

Since the date when man first appeared in North America is gradually being pushed farther and farther into the past, it may well be that some of the Indian's ancestors were on this continent before the *Homo sapiens* of the Old World diversified into Mongoloids, Negroids, and Caucasoids. If that is true, those people may belong to the oldest race on earth. Some of the purest blood types found in the world belong to the American Indi-

Menominee girl

ans, a fact which tends to substantiate the idea that they were isolated before racial mixing occurred.

People from Asia, moving southward from the ice-choked regions of the North, filtered through the western states into Mexico, while others passed into the Mississippi Valley, then over the low mountains to the woodlands of the East. Northern hunters, stalking the mastodon, probably skirted the margins of the glacier as it retreated from the Great Lakes.

An accepted date for habitation of the Northeastern woodland area—extending from the Mississippi River to the Atlantic Ocean, north into Canada and southward to present-day Kentucky—is 5,000 to 7,000 years ago, when people belonging to the Old Copper Culture lived around the Great Lakes in the present region of Wisconsin. This hunting and fishing culture lasted about 2,000 years, during which time implements were hammered out of native copper. Lance points, knives, awls, chisels, and axes of solid copper were highly valued by other eastern people with whom the Old Copper people established a trade. Canoes were probably a means of transportation between these people and their neighbors to the east—neighbors as far east as the Maritime Provinces, who were chipping slate into points and knives very similar to the kinds made out of copper by the people of the Great Lakes.

By 1000 B.C., woodland hunters from the Northwest were spreading their culture, that was based on caribou hunting, eastward across the Canadian tundra to Hudson Bay, northeastern Canada, and as far as Greenland.

At about the same time another curious group of eastern people were burying their dead in mounds, the beginning of a remarkable culture that would, for a long time, mystify scholars

Cree youth

23

Mound Builders

of modern times. Even Thomas Jefferson, who called these people Mound Builders, was so intrigued with their work that he excavated a mound in Virginia in which he discovered thousands of their bones.

From the Gulf Coast to New York State, the work of the Mound Builders can still be seen in thousands of unusual earthworks resembling giant snakes, deer, bears, turtles, and birds, geometric embankments and enclosures, or pyramids one hundred feet high. Mound building began as part of an elaborate burial ceremony in which corpses were placed on the ground with arms and legs close to their bodies and mounds of earth heaped over them. Valuable possessions were often buried with the dead, and excavations have yielded many artifacts helpful in unveiling the facts about the people who built the mounds.

The most spectacular development of the Mound Builders occurred over a thousand years before the Europeans began to explore North America. This high point, known as the Hopewell Culture, flourished in the valleys of Illinois and Ohio from 400 B.C. to 400 A.D. when it mysteriously vanished in favor of simpler living. The Hopewells invaded the territory of the Adena people, another group of mound builders who raised maize as a crop, adopted their farming techniques and established a highly developed society. Artifacts from Hopewell mounds reveal that they were importers on a large scale. Hammered copper articles show that they traded with the people of the Great Lakes. They obtained mica from the Carolinas, pearls, conchs, and other exotic shells from the coast, obsidian and grizzly bear teeth from the Rocky Mountains. They made fine pottery, woven textiles, art objects, and tools of stone, bone, wood, and copper. In one Hopewell mound a copper ax was discovered, weighing twenty-eight pounds. In another, a grave was found covered with 60,000 pearls. Still others have yielded hundreds of carved stone pipes, lifelike statuettes, and silhouettes of heads and hands expertly cut from sheets of mica. Evidently, there were social classes among the Hopewells, for only elite members of their society were given elaborate burials.

Later Mound Builders erected earthworks for reasons other then burying their dead, since for that purpose they constructed cemeteries. This culture, called Mississippian, because it centered about that river, reached a peak between 1300 and 1500 A.D. and its influence stretched even to the northern Algonkian tribes of Canada.

By the sixteenth and seventeenth centuries, the Ohio Valley supported only a few native tribes, and the white men who came upon the astonishing mounds attempted to explain them as the remains of a vanished race. Whether it was destroyed by war, revolt, famine, or disease, the great age of the prehistoric Mound Builders had faded from America before the sails of Columbus' ships were sighted from its shores.

A Woodland Indian family

The Paleo-Indians had followed different routes and made numerous cultural advances as they migrated eastward and evolved into the Woodland Indians. Some of these migrants remained as hunters and journeyed across Canada to the Northeast where they became the Algonkian Indians. These nomadic people roamed the eastern woodlands for centuries before the aggressive Iroquois moved up from the south. Other groups of prehistoric people, who had first journeyed to the southwest and then turned east, bringing maize into the Mississippi Valley, were probably the forerunners of the mysterious Mound Builders. Whether they were a remnant of the Mound Building tribes or merely casual travelers through the Mississippi and Ohio valleys, the ancestors of the Iroquois brought maize cultivation to its northern growing limits when they invaded the domain of the Algonkians. The fifteenth-century Europeans found the eastern forests inhabited by the two contenders for tribal supremacy —the Algonkians and the Iroquoians. Almost without exception, all tribes of the region belonged to one of these two large divisions of the Red Race.

Chapter 2

---◆---

THE PEOPLE OF THE
WOODLANDS

"ON THIS DAY came again the savage, and brought with him five other proper men. They had every man a deer's skin on him and the principal of them had a wild-cat's skin, or such like on the one arm. They had most of them long hose up to their groins, close made, and above their groins to their waist another leather. They were altogether like the Irish trousers. They are of complexions like our English gypsies, no hair or very little on their faces, on their heads long hair to the shoulders, only cut before, some trussed up before with a feather, broad wise, like a fan, another a fox tail hanging out. They were in their faces in part or in whole painted, some black, some red, some yellow, and some white, some with crosses, and other fanciful works. Some had skins on them and some naked, all strong, tall men in appearance. The King had at his bosom hanging on a string, a great long knife."

—from accounts of the Pilgrims at Cape Cod, 1621

These "savages" encountered by the Pilgrim fathers were among the survivors of a deadly epidemic which had raged among the coastal Algonkian Indians for several years, decimating thousands. Those religious immigrants who survived the Atlantic crossing discovered the fields at Plymouth to be already cleared, for it had once been Patuxet, an abandoned Wampanoag Indian village where disease had nearly wiped out its inhabitants. Nearby, the Pilgrims found the surviving Wampanoags, led by their grand sachem, Massasoit, to be friendly and helpful.

Verrazano, one of the earliest explorers along the New England coast, wrote this short passage in 1524 concerning the Indians of Narragansett Bay: "They are full of pity and charity for their neighbors. They are very liberal, for they give that which they have. We became great friends with these."

But not all early writings credit the Indian with a sterling character. In 1606, the explorer Champlain, in describing the Cape Cod Indians, said, "In appearance they seem to be of good disposition, but the whole of them, to tell the truth, are not worth much. The slightest intercourse with them at once discloses their character. They are great thieves, and if they cannot lay hold of a thing with their hands, try to do so with their feet, as we have repeatedly learned by experience."

With conflicting accounts it is difficult to determine what the native American was really like as a person. Firsthand reports by explorers, missionaries, and colonists, paint pictures of the Indians ranging from selfless saints to bloodthirsty fiends. Undoubtedly, examples of both could be found among the Indians as among any people. Encounters with the natives were made by various people from many places, with differing purposes and prejudices. Having little or no knowledge or understanding of the strange inhabitants of the New World, the Europeans approached the Indians with varying strategies. It is understandable that the Indian reacted in all manner of ways which were interpreted as either hostile or friendly by their visitors. Some of the early explorers found the Indians to be mild-mannered and peaceful, while later colonists had good reason to call them thieves and murderers. Those earliest encounters with the coastal tribes were mostly peaceful, since the Indians were probably as interested in the white men as the explorers were in the swarthy savages. Later meetings became less congenial as the Indian discovered that the Europeans entered his world for lands and riches. Though needed at first, the Indian gradually became an obstacle not to be tolerated in the path of conquest. The Jesuits, early missionaries in lands dominated by the Iroquoian tribes, labeled all of these people as treacherous fiends except the Hurons who aided them. Yet the Hurons were probably little different in character from their other Iroquoian relatives.

If the Europeans did not all agree on the character of the people they met, their descriptions of the Indian's appearance are less varied. The white men found the Indians larger than themselves, powerfully built, with darker skins, black eyes and hair. The sturdy savages dressed in skins, furs, or grasses, dyed and painted their bodies, and were adorned with ornaments of feathers, stones, shells, bones, leather, and copper.

The costume of the Northeastern Indian varied, depending upon the climate and the season, but generally the Woodland peoples wore similar garb. The Indian dressed in clothes to suit the variable temperatures of a changing climate. Those of the far north, where summers are very short, were clothed in well-fitting skin garments during much of the year. The women wore dresses made from two skins which hung from the shoulders down the front and back and to which sleeves could be added for extra warmth. Men wore leggings and coats like those of their Eskimo neighbors. Farther to the south the men wore little besides a breechclout and moccasins in warm weather, while the women dressed in leather skirts, leggings, and moccasins.

The breechclout or loincloth was worn by most of North America's male population. It was a strip of hide about a foot wide and several feet long which went between the legs and was held in front and back by a string about the waist. The overlapping ends, which were often decorated, hung down in front and back. The buckskin leggings, which were made in pairs but not sewn together, were about as far as the Northeastern natives got in the complicated art of trouser-making. These garments fitted over each leg and were held up by a cord which fastened the upper and outer edge to the waistband. Excess material left after an article of clothing had been made was often slashed to form fringes. To prevent them from catching in bushes, leggings had short fringes or none at all. The explorers noticed that the coastal Indians wore skirts of grasses and hemp, and robes of wild turkey feathers which were sewn to a netlike fabric so carefully that the finished cape easily shed the rain. When the chill of winter moved into the woodlands and blanketed the barren

Breechclout and leggings

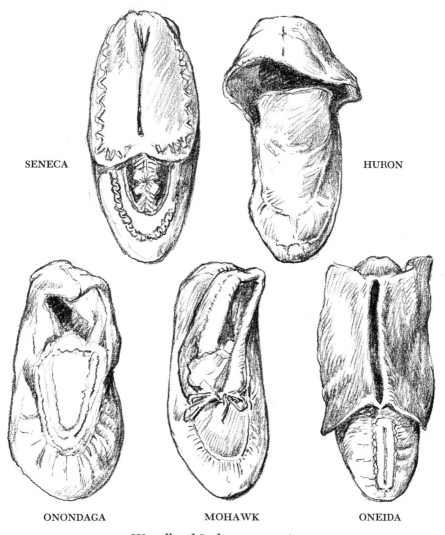

SENECA

HURON

ONONDAGA

MOHAWK

ONEIDA

Woodland Indian moccasins

ground with snow, the men added buckskin leggings and shirts, while the women wore full-length skin dresses. Coastal Indians wore skin robes across their shoulders rather than shirts. These were made from the hides of deer, wolf, wildcat, or bear. Extra fur sleeves and moccasins lined with rabbit fur were needed when the people stepped from their firesides into the frigid cold.

The moccasin, once worn by most North American natives, is a true Indian invention. Styles varied with the tribes but, unlike their western counterparts, the Northeastern Indians wore soft-soled moccasins which came up to the ankles where they were tied. The Chippewa are known for creating moccasins with puckered tops, while among the Sac and Fox the women's footgear had long side flaps reaching nearly to the ground. Many moccasins were decorated in the early days with flattened porcupine quills, as were other clothing items.

Hair styles, too, varied with the tribes of the Northeast. Women usually wore their long glossy hair in one or two braids. The Algonkian women wore ornamented "square caps" on their heads. The men also wore braids, especially the westernmost hunters of the region. A common hair style of the warrior was the roach, a ridge of stiff black hair two or three inches high, which ran from the forehead to the nape of the neck. The Sac, Fox, Menominee, and some coastal Indians wore a roach made of red-dyed deer hair. The hair along the sides of the head was plucked out, shaved, or burned off with hot stones. The scalp lock was often grown long and braided so that it hung down in back, a defiant challenge to the warrior's enemies to try to part him from his hair. Various ornaments, including shells, feathers, metal, or stones, were used as hair decorations. The Indian took great pride in his hair and often rubbed bear fat into it so that it would shine.

The Indian not only decorated his hair and clothing but wore earrings, bracelets, necklaces, tatoos, and paints to enhance his appearance. Limonite and graphite were the sources of the red and black pigments with which the Indians painted their faces. By rubbing soot into deep scratches, the Delawares tatooed their entire bodies with designs representing memorable dreams and daring exploits.

The Norsemen, whose sagas give some of the earliest descrip-

tions of coastal Indians, told of swarthy and ferocious "skrael-
ings" with ugly hair, big eyes, and broad cheeks. The American
Indians belong to the Mongoloid racial stock, as do the peoples
of eastern Asia, and although they show great intertribal variations, nearly all have certain features in common among themselves and with the Asians. The Indian women resemble the
Asiatic people more closely than do the men. The similarities are

A Micmac and Norsemen

in their high-bridged noses and prominent brow-ridges, contributing to a certain angularity of the facial features. All Indians have bluish-black or brownish-black hair, with very little on their bodies. In most cases the hair is straight or slightly wavy and does not tend toward baldness or graying. The Indians of the East are tall and often possess an aquiline nose.

A genetic relationship with the Mongoloid peoples of Asia is also exhibited in the same low frequencies of certain blood types. The Indian population differs from the Asian in that it lacks the Rh negative factor completely. Such differences, which are hereditary, may be explained by the fact that the Indians were in America before the Mongoloid type had completely evolved in Asia.

Mistakenly named "Indians" by Christopher Columbus, who believed them to be inhabitants of India, the natives of America do not have a name for themselves as a race. Most groups refer to themselves by tribal names which often mean "people" or "men." In addition to Indians, they have been called Americans, red men, redskins, savages, heathens, and many other less complimentary terms. The word "Amerind," a combination of American and Indian, was suggested by J. W. Powell, director of the Bureau of American Ethnology, as a name to replace the indefinite and confusing term "Indian." Although the word is used, it has never become popular and the native of the Americas reminds us still of an explorer's delusion as we continue to call him simply, the Indian.

Complicated by many factors, the study and classification of the North American Indian languages is not yet complete. Although possessing a rich oral literature, the Indian had no written language in the early days. With the coming of the missionaries and explorers, some of the Indian words were recorded, but this was done only to help communicate with the natives and not for purposes of linguistic study. Today many Indian languages have

POTTOWATOMI

SAC AND FOX

SHAWNEE

Algonkian Indians

disappeared or are spoken by only a few people. Others have become altered, especially by the addition of new words to compensate for contributions from the white man's culture. The linguist, deprived of recorded information about language in early America, has to work backwards, assuming that there were once certain protolanguages from which the modern Indian language families evolved. In Europe, for instance, Latin is the protolanguage from which the related French, Italian, Spanish, and Portuguese languages developed. Although there is no accurate knowledge of the number of Indian languages spoken at the time of Columbus' arrival in the New World, it is estimated that there were about three hundred languages spoken north of Mexico by about 1,500,000 Indians. Most modern Indians are bilingual, but they find less and less use for their native language in today's world. As the Indian forsakes ancestral ways it is probable that all his ancient tongues will one day become extinct. An exception to the gradual abandonment of native language is to be found among the Ojibwa or Chippewa, a northern tribe whose language has flourished rather than diminished in its use.

Although the Woodland Indians had fewer words in the vocabularies of their languages than did the Europeans, this does not suggest that their speech was simple but rather that their lives were less complicated, with fewer objects and ideas to be named. Many Indian languages are so complicated in grammatical structure that they are most difficult to learn. The Indian often finds English very indefinite, for his own language has far more expressions to describe or identify persons and things. Where in English the plural means simply more than one, Indian languages often have two plurals, one meaning things bunched together and another referring to things that are spread out. Using only two words, an Indian could distinguish a pile of collected acorns from the nuts scattered under an oak tree. As proof of the cryptic nature of Indian languages, one has only to recall that during World War II, Indians were used in the front lines to communicate secret information in their native tongues. Their languages, used in lieu of codes, could not be translated by any of the German or Japanese linguistic experts.

Through similarities in sounds, grammar, and vocabulary among some native languages, it is fairly certain that common lingual ancestors existed among the Indians of ages ago. But it is also known that the languages of the Americas are too diverse to have come from any single source. It would be convenient if the Indian tongues resembled some Asian language, but there is no clear evidence showing that any of them do.

The Indians of the Northeast represent two major linguistic families, Algonkian and Iroquoian. The Algonkians, migratory hunters and fishermen, were the original inhabitants of the region. Iroquoian-speaking people, semisedentary and semiagricultural, invaded Algonkian territory and dispersed its occupants. In the seventeenth century the Indians of the wooded north were mostly bands of constantly shifting peoples at different cultural levels with differing modes of living. By far the larger was the Algonkian-speaking group. At the time of European discovery, Algonkian was spoken across southern Canada from the Rockies to the Atlantic and south to what was later the state of Tennessee. Iroquoian tongues were spoken throughout the valley of the St. Lawrence River and around Lakes Erie and Ontario, southward to the northern part of Georgia.

The early Europeans found the Indians living throughout the forests in scattered villages, differing in many ways, but with one thing in common: whether Algonkian or Iroquois, they lived in the vast woodlands—nearly unbroken for a thousand miles—and until the arrival of the white man, depended entirely upon it for their sustenance.

The lives of Algonkians and Iroquois were different in several ways. The very fact that the Algonkians migrated in search of game, while the Iroquois lived a more settled life, indicates a contrast in the possessions and dwellings of the two peoples. The Algonkians' belongings were necessarily of a portable nature and their houses or wigwams were fairly easy to assemble or dismantle. The Iroquois, on the other hand, lived for ten or fifteen years in one village where they practiced agriculture extensively. Their palisaded villages contained larger, more substantial, multifamily dwellings. Politically, the Iroquoian way of life lent itself to a more unified organization than did the Algonkian, whose small hunting groups were spread over larger areas. Eventually, most Algonkians, too, became settled and raised a few crops or harvested those of the wilds. They constructed their simple wigwams in villages, though few of their settlements were ever stockaded as were those of the Iroquois.

Perhaps because of being more settled, with a more certain food supply, the Iroquois had more time to devote to other pursuits but, regardless of the reason, these were a people of a more warlike nature than their wigwam-dwelling neighbors. The conclusion must not be drawn that the forest was a continual battlefield. Quite contrary to this belief, even the Iroquois were more often at peace than at war. Their whole political structure was based on harmony and it was ironic that they resorted to warfare in their attempt to achieve the Great Peace. Generally, the wars —actually raids—were but small-scale affairs between feuding neighbor tribes. A tendency toward hostility and slaughter, implied by the description "warlike," was truly not a part of the Woodland Indian's character.

Concerning the Indian's character, a more misunderstood and misrepresented people would be hard to find. The Indian is often pictured standing among white men, silent and sullen, glaring at his surroundings with bitterness and contempt. This is not the portrait of the Indian who was on hand to greet the white men

CHIEF

WARRIOR

MEDICINE MAN

Iroquois Indians

in the days of earliest discovery. From many accounts one reads of the eager, innocent native, thoroughly delighted by the trinkets shown him by his visitors. Bitterness and contempt for the white man and his ways grew as a result of European encroachments, and if it is a part of Indian character today, it is not without justification.

An acceptable measure of commendable Iroquois character can be found in the qualities which the Indians themselves admired in the men who were made their chiefs. These traits included valor, dignity, sincerity, incorruptibilty, and a likeable personality. This is much the same image the modern-day political figure is anxious to present to the people who have the power to elect him to a position of leadership.

Indian values differ so markedly from those of the white man that he may appear a grim, humorless individual, while in reality being quite the contrary. Emotional control is a virtue among the Indians, who are taught from childhood to mask their feelings. Among themselves the Indians are full of humor, and the typical Indian village resounded with the cheerful clamor of dogs barking, children shouting, and people laughing. The Indian is also taught to bear pain in silence and it is considered a mark of his bravery that even while being tortured to death, he insults his tormentors and ignores his agony.

A great difference between the Indian and the white man lies in the concepts of land ownership. The white man, greedy for personal property, finds it difficult to appreciate the Indian's attitude that land is held in common. To the Indian, the land feeds, clothes, and shelters him, and he belongs to the land. Tribal property, shared by all, was a necessity in a hunting culture where a great deal of land is needed to support even one family. The Indian did not comprehend individual ownership of property, and treaties or sales of land were often violated because the Indian did not realize the full meaning of his agreements. To the Indian, the land is likened to one's mother and it goes without saying that one does not sell his mother. Stated simply, the separation between Indian and white is this: The Indian was mainly concerned with living, the white man with getting.

The Indian of the woodlands lived as a part of nature. He did not try to control his environment but, rather, to fit into it. From the forests and streams the Indian obtained material for his shelters, hides for his clothing, animals and plants for his food, and the elements for his superstition-filled religion.

Religion was a powerful factor in the life of the forest Indian. It dominated and disciplined every phase of his life. In his scheme of things, all the elements of nature were related. There dwelled a spirit in every tree, rock, and forest-bordered stream. Every awe-inspiring mystery of nature became a deity whose wrath was guarded against or goodness implored. The Indian looked not to any one Great Spirit but to the thunder, winds, echoes, sun, moon, and stars for his many gods. He existed in a world of ghosts and goblins where the powerful spirits of the dead lived close at hand. To ward off, placate, or thank the gods and spirits of his wooded domain, the Indian held elaborate feasts, carried out detailed ceremonies, and respected strong taboos. Through his primitive beliefs and rituals, the Indian found explanation and comfort for the events of his world and in his life.

Chapter 3

———◆◆———

TRIBAL LIFE OF THE
WOODLAND INDIAN

WITHIN A RUDE bark hut, the dejected family huddled close to their small fire. Hunting had gone badly again today and the tired men had returned home empty handed. If it had not been for a hot broth from the few roots the women had stored, there would have been nothing at all to eat on this frosty night. The wind howled through the dark spruce forest and around the simple shelter. Icy blasts found their way through cracks in the birchbark shingles, stirring the fire and causing it to cast weird flickering shadows upon the dimly lighted walls. The children imagined great hulking bears and giant birds with long talons moving about the inside of the wigwam, and the adults too felt the presence of spirits tonight. Little was said, for each was absorbed in his own private thoughts and fantasies. Soon they would sleep, tightly wrapped in deerskin robes with their feet toward the fire. The women added several small branches to the flames and hoped they had collected enough dry wood to last until morning. The hunters sat grim-faced, wishing that the swirling snow would stop and that tomorrow one of them might kill a deer. Then there would be meat to feed the hungry family for a while.

Throughout the gloomy northern forests similar families gathered together in primitive dwellings and struggled against the winter hardships. Food they had stored was running low, game was especially hard to find, and all looked forward to the returning spring when life would be better again.

These Woodland people were a band of Algonkian hunters roaming the northeastern forests 10,000 years before the first European set foot in the New World. Such primitive peoples moved about in small family groups, since entire tribes traveling together would be unable to find sufficient food. As with all primitive, hunting people, the family became the basic social unit. Early Algonkian tribes were loosely organized and, although respected for his wisdom, a chief had little authority over the various groups within his tribe. Ownership of land by individual tribes was recognized, even though tribal meetings were infrequent. Family groups defended their portions of tribal domain and for centuries the Algonkian people continued their ancient and, generally, peaceful way of life in an untamed wilderness.

The Algonkian tribesmen, living in scattered bands, were in an unprepared position to defend their territories when powerful invaders began moving into the eastern woodlands. The intruders were known as the Iroquois, a name adapted by the French from the Algonkian word *Irinakoiw,* meaning "real adders." The Algonkians were pushed toward the outer fringes of their old territory by these feared and hated newcomers.

The Algonkians took with them a family-centered way of life which became altered as they met the needs of survival in new environments. Those who fled eastward became the coastal Indians with whom Europeans first dealt. With food from the sea more readily available than game hunted in the forest, they were able to settle in villages from Labrador to North Carolina. Another group moved westward, abandoned their primitive

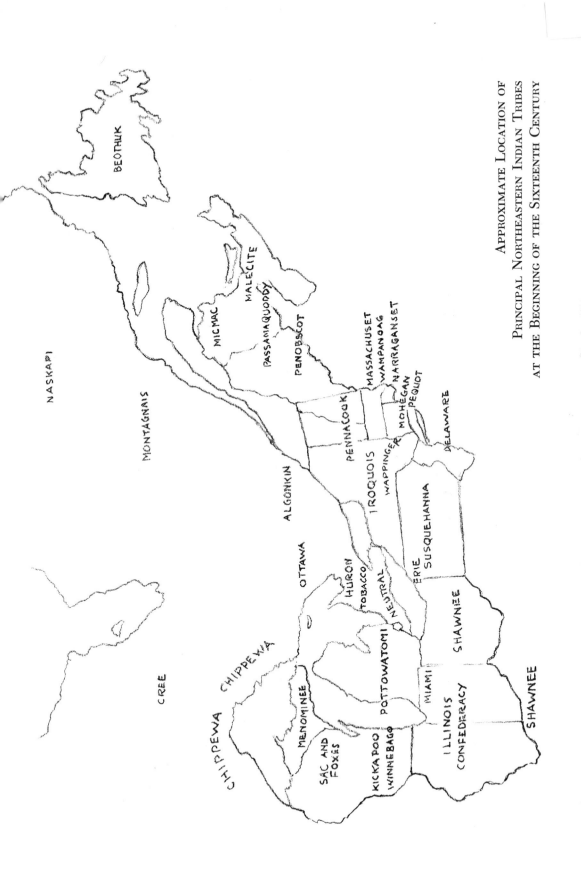

Approximate Location of
Principal Northeastern Indian Tribes
at the Beginning of the Sixteenth Century

hunting, and became a farming culture in lands which would at a later day be called Ohio and Illinois. The remainder were pushed northward and continued to live much as they always had, hunting in the woodlands of the far North.

As the Algonkians relocated themselves, they began to build settlements and to develop stronger tribal groupings. Some of their tribes are remembered for parts played in American history, others for a name given to a river, mountain, city, county, or state, and many have simply faded from memory as these Indians themselves disappeared or lost their identities.

Along the rocky shores of Nova Scotia, Cape Breton Island, and northern New Brunswick lived the Micmac Indians. Thought to be among the earliest arrivals in that area, this Algonkian tribe is said to have met with sea-roving Norsemen exploring those coasts. The Malecites lived along the southern bank of the St. Lawrence River, bordered Micmac territories within Nova Scotia and New Brunswick, and also inhabited part of Maine, the homeland of the Passamaquoddy and Penobscot tribes. The Malecites, Passamaquoddys, Penobscots, and several smaller tribes are often referred to as Abenakis, since at one time they were loosely allied. The Pennacooks of Maine, New Hampshire, and Massachusetts became known to white men as the Merrimac, after the river that cut its course through their homelands. The Massachusett Indians lived on a great coastal inlet where the city of Boston now stands. Massachusetts Bay and the state itself were named for this tribe. A smaller tribe of this region, called the Wampanoags, is remembered for its role in Pilgrim history. The Narragansett, or "People of the Small Bay," established villages in areas now a part of Rhode Island. In lands known to the natives as Quonoktacut, or "River Whose Water Is Driven by Tides," lived the Mohegans and their relatives, the Pequots. Quonoktacut, later called Connecticut, was also the home for the Wappinger tribe. Along the upper Hudson River

Mahican

in New York State lived a group known as the Mahicans, often confused with the Mohegans of Connecticut. Though the situation is complicated by variations in the spelling of the two names, both have been translated to mean "wolf," indicating that they are related.

Dominating the coast from lower New York State southward into Delaware was a powerful tribe calling themselves the Lenni Lenape or "Original People." More commonly known as the Delawares, they were named by the English for a countryman, Lord de la Warre.

Those Algonkian people who moved toward the west included a very large tribe called the Ojibway. The name is derived from a word which, in early translations, meant "to roast until puckered up" and referred to the puckered tops of their moccasins. Ojibway was mispronounced often enough so that eventually the word became Chippewa. This widespread group lived around the northern shores of Lake Huron and Lake Superior and westward to North Dakota.

Other people speaking the Algonkian language in the region of the Great Lakes included the Ottawa, a trading tribe whose name comes from a Cree word *adawe,* meaning "to buy and sell." The Ottawa, forced by the Iroquois from their homes along the Ottawa River in Canada, moved to Manitoulin Island in Lake Huron, later dispersing into what is now southern Michigan and the nearby sections of Indiana and Illinois. Also occupying parts of Michigan and the islands of northern Lake Huron were the Pottowatomi, "the fire-makers," whose name signified their custom of making a tribal council fire.

A warlike tribe, the Menominee, or "wild rice men," harvested this epicurean grain from the shallows of Wisconsin and upper Michigan lakes. The Sac or Sauk and Fox, allied in the mid-eighteenth century, joined with the neighboring Kickapoos in wars against the French and Chippewas. The Sac, known as the "Yellow Earth People" and the Fox, called the "Red Earth People," lived along the western shores of Lake Michigan. The Winnebago, although a Siouan-speaking tribe, lived much like their forest-dwelling Algonkian neighbors in Wisconsin. Their name, Winnebago, meant "People of the Filthy Water" and they became known to the English as Stinkards.

In an area to the south of Lake Michigan lived the tribes of the Illinois or Illini, who in 1673 welcomed the Jesuit, Marquette, and his companion, the explorer, Joliet. In 1682 the Illinois were visited by La Salle, which may have had further

Algonkin

influence in turning the allegiance of these Indians to the cause of the French.

North of the St. Lawrence River, in present-day Ontario, earliest French explorers were befriended by a small tribe called Algonkins. The French applied the name to many neighboring tribes as well as the Algonkins proper. The word Algonkian, referring to the whole language group, was derived from the name of this tribe. The Algonkins were later disbanded in wars with the Iroquois.

Across the northern stretches of Canada, eastward to the Plains, roamed members of a far-reaching tribe known as the Cree. The Eastern Cree were much like other northern woodland people, while the group known as the Plains Cree became bison hunters on the prairies of southern Manitoba and Saskatchewan.

The far North became the dwelling place of many related Algonkian bands, known collectively as the Montagnais and the Naskapis. In search of caribou, they ranged the subarctic wilderness of Labrador west to Hudson Bay.

Across the foggy strait from Labrador, with Eskimos as their neighbors, lived the timid, pale-skinned Beothuks, hunted like animals by early Newfoundland fishermen and later exterminated by their Micmac relatives to the south. These little-known Newfoundland Indians are believed to have met the Vikings in 1000 A.D. At the time of their discovery by other Europeans in the sixteenth century the Beothuk people numbered only about five hundred.

Algonkian dialects were spoken by such widely separated tribes as the Shawnee or "southerner" of Kentucky and the Blackfoot, Cheyenne, and Arapaho of the Plains. Some of this language family ranged as far west as California, namely the Wiyot and Yurok.

Following their expulsion of the Algonkians, the Iroquois became the inhabitants of the lower Great Lakes area and gradually spread eastward along the Mohawk Valley to the Hudson River, Lake Champlain, and the Richelieu River in Canada. They had become masters of a broad land, abundant in game and fertile soil. Though of a warlike nature, the Iroquois cleared tracts in the forest and became the first farmers of the northern woodlands.

The Iroquoian language family included many tribes, but the term Iroquois usually refers to the five tribes which lived on adjoining territories throughout central New York State and one other, the Tuscaroras, a tribe originally from North Carolina. Westernmost of the original five were the Senecas, who called themselves "People of the Mountain." The Cayuga, or "People of the Marsh," occupied the lands east of the Seneca tribe. Bordering the Cayugas were the Onondaga whose name meant "on the hill," from the location of their first stockaded village. The Oneida called themselves "People of the Stone" because close to their village was a granite boulder which was held sacred. The Oneida lands joined those of the easternmost tribe, the Mohawks, reputed to be the fiercest and most cruel of the Iroquois tribes. The Narragansetts named them Mohawk, meaning "man eaters," since they were known to eat human flesh.

Montagnais girl

Other northeastern tribes related to the Iroquois included the Susquehanna Indians of Pennsylvania and the upper Chesapeake Bay. Known as Conestogas to the English, this group was called Minquas by the Dutch. The French referred to them as Andastes, short for Andastoguehronnons, a name by which they were known to their close allies, the Hurons. The Erie or "Cat Nation" lived on the southern side of the lake to which they gave their name. Erie meant "long tail" and these Indians called themselves the "People of the Panther." North of the Great Lakes lived the Attiwandaronk or Neutrals, close kinsmen of the

53

Eries and trading partners of the neighboring Hurons. They earned the name "Neutral" when they remained out of the fighting between the Hurons and the Five Nations. The aristocratic Hurons were middlemen in trade between the French and other northern tribes. The name Huron comes from a French word meaning "bristly head." An agricultural tribe living near the Hurons was the Tionontati or "Tobacco Nation." These people raised hemp, maize, and sunflowers in addition to the tobacco for which they were named. The Hurons so dominated their economy that the Tionantati became known as Tobacco "Hurons."

The Iroquois way of life centered around a fortified village containing a number of long houses. The several families living together in a long house were members of the same clan. All the families in a particular clan could trace their descent to a common ancestor. Women headed the Iroquois families and it was through the women that descent was always traced. For instance, a child belonged to the Deer Clan if his mother was of that lineage and when he grew to manhood and married, his children would be of the clan from which his wife had come.

A clan took its name from an animal which then became its totem or guarding spirit. By legend there were two original clans, the Deer and the Wolf. From the Deer Clan came the Snipe, the Heron, and the Hawk, and from the Wolf Clan came the Bear, the Beaver, and the Turtle Clans.

An Iroquois myth tells of the beginning of the Turtle Clan. In early times there were many mud turtles living in a small lake, which dried up during a very hot summer, forcing the turtles to move to a new home. One of them, a very fat and lazy turtle, was unaccustomed to walking and suffered from blisters under his shell. After much discomfort he finally, with a mighty effort, threw off his shell and was shortly thereafter transformed into a man. According to the ancient tale, he was the progenitor of the Turtle Clan.

Clans were in turn grouped into two larger divisions called *moieties* or *phratries* which then made up the tribe. Each moiety contained a number of clans which were related in a specified way. In the Seneca tribe, one moiety included the clans named for the four-footed animals except the Deer, and the other moiety included the Deer and all the clans named for birds. One was not allowed to marry a member of his own moiety, just as marriage between the original Deer and Wolf Clans had been taboo. This system worked well because it avoided marriages between blood relatives.

Some of the Algonkian peoples, now organized into tribes, managed to form some intertribal confederations and as with the Iroquois, they also had clans within their tribes.

It is known that the Delaware Indians of the Atlantic seacoast were divided into three clans—Unalachtigo, Unami, and Munsee—more easily spoken of as Turkey, Turtle, and Wolf.

Among the Chippewa Indians, whose ancestors were driven westward by the Iroquois, there are more than twenty clans. One modern Chippewa legend of the Crane Clan reflects a bit of their history subsequent to leaving the East. In the early days, the Great Spirit ordered the crane to fly down to earth in search of a good place for people to live. As the bird neared the earth it saw the Great Lakes and chose to live at the place where the waters of Lake Superior meet the waters of Lake Huron. The hill on which the crane first settled is near the present town of Sault Sainte Marie in Michigan. Other animals heard the crane calling and came to live nearby. People who made homes near the crane became known as the Crane Clan. Other people took the names of their closest animal neighbors—Bear, Catfish, Loon, Moose, and Marten.

For a long time everyone was happy and then the crane became restless and began to search for a new home. It flew to the northwestern shore of Lake Superior. When the crane landed and called out, its cry was answered by the loon, which had fol-

The crane chooses the Great Lakes

lowed it. According to the Crane Clan, this legend proves their claim that they were the first to settle near Sault Sainte Marie and this is why they were the first to speak at Chippewa council meetings. The Loon, because it followed the crane and answered its call, speaks second.

Historically, the Chippewa did live for a time on Michigan's upper peninsula. Although they were once united with the Ottawa and Pottowatomi tribes, the Chippewa moved farther west as their fur trade with Europeans expanded.

In another version of this story, two cranes were sent to earth. When they discovered the outlet of Lake Superior teeming with fish, they decided to make it their home. Folding their wings close to their sides, they were changed into a man and a woman. It is said that the Crane Clan descended from the children of the two cranes.

The histories of the northeastern Indians reveal that a number of confederacies were established, often for military or defense purposes. Although several Algonkian tribes did form confederacies, they never developed a political system as functional as that of their Iroquois neighbors.

In the years before the white men came to settle in North America, the Iroquois tribes had lived independently of one another and were ruled by councils with members elected from each clan. Besides terrorizing nearby Algonkians, they often waged war on one another. Blood feuds were a common cause for wars, since they were easily started, sometimes by accident, and once begun, they became self-perpetuating. If a Cayuga killed a Seneca tribesman, the Senecas took revenge by murdering a member of the Cayuga tribe. It was not simply an eye for an eye, however, because now the Cayugas had a new murder to avenge and they in turn killed another Seneca. To worsen matters, Algonkians often took advantage of these situations and attacked Iroquois villages while the warriors were away carrying on a feud.

Shortly before the European arrivals on Indian lands, a prophet called Dekanawida arose among the Iroquois. He envisioned a "Great Peace" by which all Iroquois tribes would live in harmony and stand united against their common enemies.

Hiawatha, a Mohawk chief—in no way related to the well-known character in Longfellow's poem—is generally given the credit for putting the prophet's ideas into practice. He is said to have founded the Five Nations, about 1570, preaching that this League of the Iroquois or Iroquois Confederacy was to be a brotherhood based on law and order. He traveled among the Iroquois villages trying to abolish feuding and the horrible practice of cannibalism.

Longfellow's Hiawatha just happened to be an adventurous Algonkian hero known to the Chippewa as Menabozho. It has long been a source of confusion that the name of the famous Iroquois statesman and reformer was mistakenly given to the Chippewa deity by the unsuspecting Longfellow.

Hiawatha had some difficulties in establishing the League, one of the most frustrating of which was the position of the stubborn Onondaga chief, Todadaho. At the time of the League's formation, Todadaho was so powerful that he was even feared by his own tribesmen. His name is translated to mean "He Whose House Blocks the Path" and his opposition to the League was certainly the main obstacle to Iroquois unity. In order to get the Onondagas to join with the other nations it was necessary to accede to the terms that Todadaho dictated. As a result, the Onondagas were given more Council representatives than any other tribe in the League. Todadaho became the ruling chief, with an exclusive right to summon a meeting of all the Council members and the Onondaga village became the capital of the Five Nations.

An Iroquois legend says that the first Todadaho was a monster whose thoughts came out of his head in the form of snakes and when he finally joined the League it was Hiawatha who combed the serpents out of his hair.

The League, as it was established, became a political enlargement of an already well-ordered society. The Five Nations—

An Iroquois

Mohawk, Oneida, Onondaga, Cayuga, and Seneca—were the large entities, but the clan still remained the basic social unit. Each tribe remained independent in the internal affairs of its own government and the League acted only in cases of intertribal concern. To do this, fifty chiefs or sachems were elected from certain "noble" families belonging to the clans within the tribes. The founders' names are carried on to this day and are used as titles of office as we use the terms Mayor or Governor. Member chiefs were replaced by persons having their same line of descent. The present Todadaho of the League is able to trace his lineage back, over four hundred years, to the original Todadaho. A chief's successor assumed not only his name, but his duties as well and was presented with a set of deer horns symbolic of a member's position. Since descent was traced through the women in a family it was the headwoman's duty to choose replacement candidates for the Council. The headwoman was obliged to get the approval of the other women of her clan, then the chiefs of her moiety, the chiefs of the opposite moiety, and finally, the Council of the League. The headwoman also had the power to depose the council member if, after three warnings, she felt he was not competent in performing his duties. Removal from the Council involved the taking away of a member's badge of office and was known as "dehorning." The headwoman accomplished this task by first placing the deer horns upon the head of the unsatisfactory chief and then ceremoniously removing them.

Another group of chiefs, known as the "Solitary Pine Trees," held positions gained by merit rather than heredity. They occupied their honorary places on the Council for life but were not replaced when they died. Hiawatha is supposed to have been rewarded with this office because of his outstanding intellect.

The organization of the League was symbolic because it was structured like an imaginary long house with each part occupied by one of the five nations much as families occupied an actual long house. Since the Iroquois territory lay in an east-west direction from the Great Lakes to the Hudson Valley, with each tribe inhabiting adjacent sections, it followed that the Mohawks became the "Keepers of the Eastern Door" and the Senecas the "Keepers of the Western Door." The Onondagas, in the center, were the "Keepers of the Council Fire" and the "Keepers of the Wampum Belts." The organization also served to reinforce the feeling of unity inherent in the idea of dwelling together in one house.

There is a legend about the League's formation which tells how a tall pine tree was taken out of the ground in the Onondaga village while the chiefs of the Five Nations threw their

Kickapoo

weapons into the hole, (probably the origin of "burying the hatchet"). The tree was then replaced and became known as the Peace Tree. Dekanawida is said to have dreamed of such a tree, having the Five Nations as its roots and an eagle perching in its upper branches watching for anyone who would disturb the peace.

The system was large, the territory it included was immense, and it was far from the smooth-running ideal envisioned by its founders. In some cases, tribes acted independently in matters where the Council should have made a decision. In other cases, warrior chiefs, who because of lineage had not qualified for council seats, acted on their own and raided other tribes.

The League did keep peace within the Five Nations and, regardless of many shortcomings, it was the best native achievement in the area of defense that had ever been made. The Five Nations easily triumphed over weaker tribes, subjugating or destroying them. It was a unique organization in that it often adopted captives and whole tribes. By doing this it replaced those who had died in battle and often increased its numbers.

European interruption of the League's growth is significant because, had it come later, the Iroquois might have had an Indian Empire so vast that history could easily have taken another course. The white men arrived before the League was at its peak, although it was in control of the lands from the Ottawa River in Canada south into Tennessee and from Maine westward to Lake Michigan. Even though unity was increased in the face of their common white enemy, the power of the Five Nations gradually decreased as the European population expanded.

The famous League of the Iroquois was the most remarkable of the Indian Confederations in the Northeast, but it was not the only one of any importance. The Huron were once a strong federation of four Iroquoian tribes—the Bear, Deer, Rock, and Cord, all bitter enemies of their Five Nations relatives. Their Confederacy was called Wendat, meaning "Dwellers on a Peninsula," and descendants of the Hurons became known as Wyandots, a variation of the original word.

The Hurons were defeated by the Iroquois, along with the Tobacco Nation, the Neutrals, the Cat Nation, and the Susquehanna. The League adopted many of these vanquished peoples into their tribes, but only the Tuscarora were ever given equal status as a Nation. After having lost their fight with the white settlers who moved into their lands, the Tuscarora left North Carolina and settled with the Oneida in New York. In 1753 they were officially made the Sixth Nation of the Iroquois.

The Lake Superior Chippewa, the Pottowatomi, and the Ottawa tribes joined in an eighteenth-century league known as the "Three Fires." It was only through their unified opposition that they were able to protect their valuable rice-growing lands from Dakota and Fox invaders.

The Illinois Confederacy included six small tribes—the Cahokia, Kaskaskia, Michigamea, Moingwena, Peoria, and Tamaroa. These Indians, traditional allies of the French, were hostile to all English settlers. The Ottawa nearly exterminated the Illinois in revenge for the murder of their famous chief, Pontiac, by a Kaskaskia Indian.

The most important Algonkian Confederacy was that of the Delaware. These Indians befriended William Penn, founder of Pennsylvania, and made several treaties with him which they kept until he died. In 1720 the Delawares accepted domination by the Iroquois in exchange for protection from the white men. In return, the Delaware tribesmen were forced to live like women and children, totally dependent upon their masters, for the Iroquois allowed no warriors among its subjugated tribes. Understandably, the Delaware were one of the few tribes to ever agree voluntarily to the "Great Peace."

Two lesser-known Indian alliances of those established along the Atlantic seacoast by Algonkian tribes included the Wabanaki Confederacy and the Wappinger Confederacy. The Wabanaki Confederacy was made up of the people known as Abenakis, namely the Malecites, Micmacs, Passamaquoddys, Penobscots, Norridgewocks, and possibly the Sokokis of Maine's Saco River. Though informally organized, this northern coastal group allied itself with the French against the English colonists and the Iroquois. The Wappinger Confederacy, relatives of the Delawares, consisted of a number of small tribes whose villages were to be found from Connecticut to the area of present-day New York City. One of these member tribes, the Manhattans, sold the island site of that city to the Dutch for the bargain price of twenty-four dollars.

Chapter 4

DWELLINGS IN THE FOREST

A FEW GRAY-BLUE wisps of smoke floated above the roofs of the rectangular, bark-covered lodges. Here and there groups of dark-skinned children scampered over sleeping dogs and around their busy mothers. Within the palisaded town, happy shouts of carefree youngsters were mingled with the good-natured grumblings of men eager to be finished with their work. The addition they were building neared completion and several of the older boys looked forward to a ball game before evening. Ten families already lived in the head matron's great house and soon her newly married daughter would bring a husband to live in the new extension. The framework was in place, its forked posts supporting horizontal poles to which bent saplings had been securely lashed. Little remained but the monotonous task of fastening each elm bark shingle to the poles.

No windows illuminated the interior of the building, but sunlight streamed in through the wide-open doorway and slanting rays filtered through the smoke holes high above. In one patch of sunshine a baby played while an older sister watched from farther down the long earthen-floored passageway. From cross-rafters above her head hung strips of dried pumpkins, strings of apples and herbs, and ears of corn, stored in anticipation of the approaching winter. Platforms piled with skins and fur robes ran along both walls, where open alcoves marked each family's allotment of living space.

Here in the stockaded safety of the Indian village Iroquois people carried on one of the traditions of their ancestors. Using the knowledge passed down from preceding generations, the natives employed their skills in the building of sturdy and practical homes.

The Iroquois dwelling was known as a long house, or *ganonh 'sees,* and although the men were responsible for its construction, a house was the property of the women. Depending upon its length, a long house accommodated from five to twenty families. The long dimension of these barnlike buildings ranged from thirty to two hundred feet, but an average lodge was about sixty feet long and eighteen feet in width. The Iroquois home was a comparatively tall building, as well as lengthy, and measured as much as twenty feet from floor to ridge pole. The roof of a long house was often triangular-shaped, although rounded roofs on many of these buildings gave them the general appearance of a modern Quonset hut.

The long house buildings of the Iroquois varied little, until the coming of the white man when many Indians adopted European house designs and furnishings. The primitive long house was simply a two-doored latticed framework covered with bark. Upright posts were first set into the ground forming an outline of the building and to these were affixed the horizontal poles and then the roof frame. Flattened sections of bark, which were collected in the spring or early summer, were fastened to the windowless walls with tough strips of inner bark from the basswood tree. Elm bark was preferred as shingling material in Iroquois lands where the birch tree was uncommon. Hemlock, basswood, ash, and cedar were substituted where elm was unavailable. The woody panels were cut into sections about four

Iroquois long house, exterior and interior

by six feet, flattened with weights, and laced to the walls through holes made in the slabs with bone punchers. Secondary poles lashed against the outer wall clamped the clapboards tightly. The doorways at both ends of the building could be closed with a piece of hide or bark. When inclement weather made it necessary, pieces of bark were also pushed across the smoke holes with long poles. When the smoke from the fires could not readily escape, the atmosphere within the long house became extremely uncomfortable and the occupants were forced to lie on the floor in order to breathe.

Small central fireplaces served one or more families and were sources of heat and light as well as cooking facilities. Each family lived in a booth from six to twelve feet in length and about six feet wide. These compartments had one platform for sleeping and another about seven feet from the ground where household goods were kept, including clothing, cooking utensils, hunting equipment, and a variety of personal possessions. Things of great value were placed in a pit which was dug under the family sleeping bench. Skin curtains afforded some privacy for each family, but few secrets were kept in an abode of this kind.

Both rounded and gable-roofed buildings might be found in the same Iroquois village, as well as several smaller dome-shaped huts. These latter structures were used for sweat baths during the summer.

When the French explorers reached the lands of the Iroquois, they were impressed by the stockades which protected the Indian villages. These forts were built from trees which the Iroquois felled by a burning and scraping technique. Fallen trees were burned through to form logs which the Indians hauled to a location and propped upright by piling earth at the bases. Usually a stronghold had two gates, one in the front for general use and a rear exit through the palisade for getting water.

Iroquois dwellings changed after the white man arrived and

Squaw building a wigwam

by Revolutionary times the long house contained many furnishings, including cornhusk rugs. Single-family dwellings became common among many of the once communal-living people, and by the dawn of the eighteenth century the long house was all but abandoned.

Many Algonkian peoples lived in dome-shaped huts known as wigwams. "Wigwam," an Abenaki word, became commonly used by white men when referring to any similarly shaped Indian dwelling. Unlike the more structurally complicated long house, a wigwam was built by women from long, thin saplings bent into semicircles and set into the ground. The arched framework was covered with available materials, including birchbark, animal skins, cornhusks, and various reeds or grasses woven into mats. The single entrance was barely three feet high but

Chippewa dwellings

the center of the structure's interior was of a height tall enough for a man to stand upright. Many wigwams must have been quite large, for the explorer Verrazano wrote this of some he saw along the New England coast: "The father and the whole family dwell together in one house in great number: In some of them we saw 25 to 30 persons."

Both the doorway and the smoke hole in the roof could be closed with a skin or mat and, in some cases, the interior walls of the wigwam were also faced with woven mats. In the center of the wigwam an arrangement of stakes over the fire held cooking pots and food to be roasted. A pit was dug to hold the fire, thereby preventing flying sparks from igniting the dry walls of the dwelling. The only furniture within the Algonkian home was a bench a few feet from the floor and running around the inside wall. Mats covered this low shelf whereon people sat or slept. Horizontal poles in the roof held strings of dried food and baskets. Other typical household goods are described in an account made by the Pilgrims after visiting wigwams near Cape Cod:

"In the houses we found wooden bowls, trays and dishes,

A Winnebago structure

earthen pots, hand-baskets made of crab-shells wrought together, also an English pail or bucket; it wanted a bail, but it had two iron ears. There were also baskets of sundry sort, bigger, and some lesser, finer, and some coarser. Some were curiously wrought with black and white in pretty works, and sundry other of their household stuff. We found also two or three deer heads, one whereof had been newly killed for it was still fresh. There was also a company of deers' feet stuck up in the houses, harts' horns, and eagles' claws, and sundry such like things. There were also two or three baskets full of parched acorns, pieces of fish, and a piece of a broiled herring. We found also a little silk grass, and a little tobacco seed, with some other seeds which we knew not. Outside were sundry bundles of flags, and sedge, bullrushes, and other stuff to make mats."

The Chippewa wigwam was well suited to the life of that traveling Algonkian tribe. A typical Chippewa home measured fourteen by twenty feet and accommodated eight people. It was covered with birchbark strips about twenty feet long and a yard wide, which could be rolled up and carried from one place to another. A woman could erect a Chippewa wigwam and have her household in running order in less than a day.

In the center of many Algonkian villages a long round-roofed building, similar to the Iroquois long house, was constructed as a meeting place or for ceremonial purposes. Larger square or rectangular bark buildings such as these were often used as summer homes by several related families. Instead of small smoke holes, a long slot in the roof served to let out the smoke from the fires.

The hunters of the North, including the Abenakis, built a tipi-shaped home. This primitive cone was about ten feet high with a diameter of the same measurement. It was covered with birch-bark held in a double frame of strong poles lashed together at the ends. These homes were more easily transported than the typical wigwams. The Crees of the westerly regions adopted a skin-covered tipi from the Plains Indians which was truly portable.

The Sac and Fox lived in large bark-covered buildings much like those of the Iroquois, but only during the summer months. These differed from the Iroquois long houses in that they were not partitioned even though many families occupied them. In the winter the Sac and Fox moved into low, oblong houses which could be more easily heated. Some of their houses were of circular shape, about fifteen feet in diameter, but the domed roof rarely exceeded six feet. Layers of mats woven from cattail rushes helped to keep out the cold winter winds. A doorway at the side permitted entry into the squat building wherein there were no platforms but beds of boughs close to the ground and around the central fireplace.

Many types of summer homes and shelters existed and most Algonkians had two or more habitats because they were more nomadic than the Iroquois peoples. Some Algonkian shelters were really camps used for short periods—at maple sugaring time, during rice harvesting season, or on hunting and fishing trips.

Shelter for the Woodland Indian was but one of his needs and probably the least troublesome. With the materials from the forest so readily available, the Indian was able to construct a suitable home, even for winter use, with little difficulty. Needs of greater prominence occupied the greater part of the Algonkian and Iroquoian people's time. The problem of a year-round food supply presented the woodland hunter and farmer with the tasks of obtaining and preserving meats and vegetables. The yearly variations in temperature required the making of suitable types of clothing to accommodate the seasonal changes. Aside from shelter, food, and clothing, the Indian designed and made the equipment and tools with which he built shelter, procured food, and fashioned his garments.

73

Chapter 5

———————•◆•———————

PROVIDING FOR THE
NEEDS OF LIFE

A LEGEND of the Hudson Bay Indians tells of a world in which there was no light, fire, or water except within the dwelling of one old chief. All the other Indians, who suffered in the cold and darkness, begged the chief for these things, but he would give them none.

At last, the Indians turned to the animals for help. To bring forth light, the animals held a dance around the stubborn chief's house and each sang a song. A faint glow was seen in the East, but the old man immediately ran out and drove it away. The animals continued their singing until the light reappeared. The chief had not slept at all and was so weary of the animals' songs that he told them they could have all the light they wanted. Now there is light every morning and to this day some animals call for the dawn.

Still the Indians did not have fire or water, so a young caribou volunteered to try to get some of the fire from the old man's home. The Indians tied some dry branches to the caribou's antlers and the animal reached its head into the chief's house in an attempt to kindle the twigs. The caribou was unable to reach the fire, but the old man was so busy driving the unwelcome visitor from his house that a clever muskrat was able to creep up to the fire and take a burning coal in its mouth. As the muskrat was running away through the woods, the coal began to burn its mouth, causing the little animal to drop the glowing ember, setting the forest aflame, and giving everyone fire. The heat from the great fire melted the ice from the lakes and rivers, providing the people with water from then on. The old chief disappeared into the forest and was never seen again.

The making and uses of fire, a knowledge brought by the Paleo-Indian in his journey from Asia, was basic to the life of all American Indians and was employed by the people of the Northeast in many ways. Needed not only as a source of heat and light, fire was used for cooking and preserving foods, tanning hides, felling trees, and hollowing out logs for use as canoes or containers.

The bountiful lands of the Northeast provided the forest-dwelling peoples with every requirement for life. In addition to building materials, the woodlands offered its animals and plants to the Indian, who had the knowledge and skills to obtain and use these gifts from nature for his food and clothing.

The earliest men to migrate to the Northeast were hunters and for some of their descendants the hunt remained a basic way of life. In addition to the gathering of wild plants, the Algonkians of the far North depended upon the deer and caribou for food and clothing. Others, such as the Iroquoian tribes, took advantage of the longer growing season of their more southern latitudes and cultivated food crops. Many Algonkian tribes living near the Iroquois and along the coast adopted agricultural practices as a supplement to hunting and fishing. All the forest people were hunters to some extent, since animal hides were needed for clothing and because wild game was their only source of meat. None of the northeastern Indians herded or raised ani-

Fishing through the ice

mals until the introduction of domesticated livestock by Europeans.

The hunt was the primary endeavor of the men of the Northeast, who in spring and summer fished the many streams and lakes and in the autumn undertook long expeditions in search of game. The animals they hunted were caribou, deer, moose, elk, and bear. When they were unable to find large game, smaller forest animals and birds were taken. These included porcupines, raccoons, woodchucks, muskrats, beaver, geese, ducks, swans, and grouse.

In the early days, fish were plentiful throughout the clean, sparkling waters of the forest and in the salty inlets of the sea. Poised on a mossy, overhanging bank, the bronze-skinned fisherman readied his bow and arrow as he watched the clean, unrippled water of a river pool for the flash of a silvery trout. Sometimes he used a three-pronged spear instead of a bow and arrow to harpoon an unwary fish. At night he paddled out onto a still lake with a companion to spear fish attracted by the light of his bark torch. Quantities of fish were caught in weirs, seines, gill nets, and other traps constructed across rivers and streams in migrating seasons. Most of the fishing was done by Algonkian people, who considered fish a much more important food than did the Iroquois.

The Algonkians of the Great Lakes region caught the awesome plated sturgeon as this ancient king of fishes combed the shallows for its food. In winter, fur-clad fishermen dangled lures through holes in the thick ice to attract *namaycush*, the lake trout, which they then speared. Other fish caught by these practiced northern fishermen included the mighty muskellunge and the landlocked salmon.

For a very large part of their menu, the coastal Indians depended upon shellfish. Evidence of this is still to be found in the great numbers of shell heaps seen all along the Atlantic coast and on the banks of salt rivers such as the Hudson. Oysters, clams, and mussels, as well as salt-water fish were eaten by all of the coastal tribes who fished the inlets and bays but seldom if ever ventured out into deeper ocean waters.

The principal weapon of the Woodland hunter was the bow and arrow and, though marksmanship was important, the Indian used many other skills in pursuit of the wary forest animals. Large animals like the stately moose and caribou were difficult to kill with one stone-tipped arrow and the wounded game often escaped into the woods. Whenever possible the hunter tried to

An Algonkian hunter

drive these animals into deep water where they could be pursued by canoe and then shot while they swam. In winter, animals floundering in deep snow could be overtaken by archers on snowshoes. The clever hunter was a skillful stalker, silent, keen-eyed, and mindful of animal instincts and habits. He knew how to lure animals toward him by imitating their calls. Sometimes he camouflaged himself beneath skins and waited for his quarry along the animal trails or at drinking places. At other times he used snares or traps to catch his game. Large hunting parties frightened deer herds toward fences they had erected, forcing the animals to jump the barriers where they could be speared by men on the opposite side.

Except for the initial clearing of land for fields, raising vegetables was a task left to women and children. They were responsible for planting, tending, and harvesting crops, as well as gathering wild plants and preparing all the foods the tribe raised, hunted, or collected.

Both Algonkian and Iroquoian peoples regarded corn or maize as a great gift and an important food crop. Although the Chippewa were not raisers of corn, they have a legend which tells how the Indians first got this valuable grain. The Chippewa say that a great hunter called Wunaumon once lived in the land. One day, after walking through the woods, he came upon a great prairie where he met a stranger who offered him a peace pipe.

The stranger was shorter than Wunaumon and did not wear deerskin but a stiff shiny coat and a red feather in his hair. The man would not tell Wunaumon his name, saying instead, "Tomorrow we will wrestle and if you win I will tell you my name and give you a gift for all your people."

Both Wunaumon and the stranger were very strong and their battle lasted from sunrise to sunset. Wunaumon saw the sun going down and thought it was ashamed of his weakness. He suddenly grew very strong and conquered the stranger, demanding to know the man's name.

"My name is Mondahmin and my body is my gift to you. Cover me with dust where we have wrestled and come back often, for you will see me again." Wunaumon did as the stranger had told him and when he returned to the place where he had buried Mondahmin there were two green feathers waving above the hill he had made.

A voice sang out to Wunaumon, saying, "This is corn, the gift of Mondahmin. Watch over this plant and take its seeds to your people. Tell them to make a feast to Mondahmin." Wunaumon brought the corn to his people and the provident gift of Mondahmin saved them from starvation.

Among the Iroquois, corn was the main item in the diet and it was so important to these people that they called it "our life." This plant, developed ages ago from some wild grain, and eventually cultivated as a crop, spread from Central America, through our Southwest, and along river trade routes until it reached the Northeast. It is believed that the Iroquois were the northward carriers of maize cultivation and that they introduced it to the Algonkians. Grown together with squash and beans, these vegetables were called "the three sisters," and the Iroquois believed that these maidens were a trio of protective spirits watching over their food crops.

The Indian farmers of the woodlands used primitive agricultural techniques. Fields were cleared by ringing trees to kill them, then burning the trunks and scraping away the charred wood with stone axes. Fields were used for several plantings and then abandoned for up to twenty years. Wooden sticks fashioned into spades were used by the women to break the ground and pile the earth into small hills where the seeds of the maize were planted.

Since the Indians attributed the growth of plants to supernatural causes, it was their custom to hold feasts in honor of particular crop-controlling spirits. Corn was so important to the Iroquois that a festival was connected with each stage of its cultivation. A planting festival was held when the seeds were sowed, another feast given when the ears of corn turned green, and a gathering festival marked the time to give thanks for an abundant harvest.

The Iroquois raised several kinds of corn, sixty varieties of beans, and eight different squashes. These vegetables were the "supporters of life," believed to have been given to the Indians by the Creator. Just as some Algonkian tribes tell of Mondah-min, the Iroquois have their own legends about the origin of

Clearing land for corn fields

certain plants. One of these stories tells of a young woman, the mother of the good and evil twins of Seneca mythology, from whose buried body five important plants grew—tobacco from her head, corn from her breast, squash from her abdomen, beans from her fingers, and potatoes from her toes. Other plants commonly cultivated by the Indians of the Northeast were cranberries, strawberries, sunflowers, and pumpkins.

The Indians also depended upon wild plants for some of their food. They ate several kinds of mushrooms, and many wild fruits, nuts, and certain leaves. After the first frost, which loosened the nuts from the trees, the women and children went about collecting acorns, hickory nuts, black walnuts, butternuts, hazelnuts, and chestnuts, which they added to corn meal or used as sources of oil. The Pottowatomi Indians used their knowledge of animal habits to aid them in collecting beechnuts. Knowing that the deer mouse gathers, shells, and stores the nuts for its winter eating, the Indians waited until the first snow and then searched out the storage places of these little animals.

Berries were eaten both raw and cooked, or were dried for winter use. Among the wild berries eaten by the Indians were strawberries, currants, chokecherries, Juneberries, blueberries, elderberries, raspberries and blackberries. Many wild plants were made into beverages. Besides water, the Iroquois Indians made twelve different drinks. One of these, a coffee-like brew, was made from roasted corn. Another was made from sunflower seeds, and tea was made by boiling the roots of the sassafras tree. Drinks were made from most berries and a popular summer beverage much like lemonade was prepared, using the velvety berries of the staghorn sumac.

A favorite wild food of many Woodland Indians was the yellow lotus, the roots of which were stored and eaten like potatoes in the winter. A pond lily known as spatterdock, also esteemed for its edible roots, was usually collected by invading the homes of muskrats where the animals had stored the roots for their own winter use. Jack-in-the-pulpit bulbs, and parts of the cattail and milkweed were also gathered for use in cooking various dishes.

Among the Algonkian Indians of the Great Lakes region the most important food was rice, the seed of a shallow water grass. This they harvested from its marshy fields in the fall, just before the grain was ripe.

Families or groups of families came to their particular rice fields several weeks before the grain ripened. About ten days before the rice was ready for gathering, women poled canoes through the beds and tied the rice stalks together. This procedure not only helped stake out harvesting territories, but also protected the crop from wind, rain, and various water birds.

The rice was harvested by bending the stalks over the boat and beating them with sticks, causing the grains to fall into the bottom of the canoe. After the rice was gathered it was dried in the sun and then placed in a hole lined with animal skins. Here the kernels were stamped on to loosen the hulls, after which they were winnowed on a large birchbark tray. The winnowed rice was washed and ready for immediate use or for storage. Most of the harvest was stored for winter provision, since rice was the primary food of tribes such as the Chippewa and Menominee.

The Indians of the woodlands used several seasonings, but although salt was obtainable it was seldom used. The Onondaga never used salt because it was tabooed. Instead, wild onions and wild ginger were used, in addition to the very popular maple sugar with which the Indians cooked almost all their dishes.

The Woodland Indians were very fond of maple sugar and began to collect sap as soon as the spring days became warm enough so that the liquid started to flow within the maple trees. Usually in early March the families moved to their grove of maple trees where they had a sugaring camp. Everyone worked

Harvesting wild rice

very hard but with gay spirits, for sugaring time meant that winter was over and the warm seasons were ahead.

The men set about repairing the camp and the large basswood vats for storing the raw syrup. The women washed the birchbark collecting pails and sealed any cracks with pitch. V-shaped gashes in the trees directed the sap toward a spout made of elder. Pails into which the liquid dripped were emptied into the vats, which had to be kept in the shade to prevent the sap from souring. To make maple sugar, the sap was boiled for many hours over a slow fire and the scum skimmed off the top. When it thickened, the liquid was poured into molds where it hardened. Syrup was made by boiling the sap for a shorter time. The children found great delight in testing the readiness of the syrup by pouring it on the snow where it hardened into delicious candy. Sour sap was a kind of vinegar used in the preparation of venison and even as a beverage on occasion.

A major problem faced by all the northern Indians was survival during the long, cold, and snowy months when hunting and food gathering were difficult. During the milder seasons much time had to be spent making clothing and preserving food in preparation for winter.

Food was preserved both by drying and smoking. Large quantities of mature corn were braided together and hung to dry both inside and outside the Indian home. The Iroquois built cribs of wooden slats for drying and storing corn. Squash and pumpkins were preserved by removing the seeds and rinds and cutting the remainder into inch-thick spirals which were hung alongside the corn.

The Iroquois made bark barrels which they buried in the ground and used for the storage of dried beans, fruits, meat, and charred corn. They also dug storage pits which were lined with bark and covered with a bark roof.

The many animals hunted by the Woodland Indians provided most of the materials needed to fashion clothing. Animal hides were scraped, tanned, cut, and sewed into garments. To accomplish these tasks, various tools and materials had to be manufactured—wood, stone, and bone scrapers, and knives, sharp needles, and strong threads. The outer rind of the milkweed plant was used as a source of fine thread with which the Indians sewed or made fishing lines. Indian hemp was also used to make very strong threads for sewing.

In addition to the basic food and clothing requirements of the Indians, many other articles were needed for use in homemaking, handicrafts, hunting, fishing, and farming. A multitude of necessities, including cooking utensils, baskets, bags, jars, and other containers of all sorts, gardening implements, weapons, ropes, nets, traps, snowshoes, and canoes, all had to be made by the Indian. Besides his necessities, the Indian made masks, pipes, toys, musical instruments, equipment for his various games, and articles solely decorative.

Until the coming of the white man, the Algonkians and Iroquois carried on their very ancient crafts in the making of all the articles for their needs and pleasures. Then the introduction of new materials revolutionized much of the Indians' handicrafts and they abandoned most of their old materials in favor of the novel European ones.

Chapter 6

———— ⚬◆⚬ ————

HOME INDUSTRY, ARTS, AND HANDICRAFTS

PATCHES OF SHIFTING fog crept among the tall, dark spruce trees and drifted into a little Abenaki village, shrouding its bark huts in a gray mist. Cold Atlantic waves broke against the rocky shore and a damp, salty breeze accompanied the rising tide.

Within the town, industrious villagers busied themselves with various tasks. A woman knelt before the low doorway of her wigwam, grinding corn between two stones, while her daughter sat nearby carefully sewing flattened porcupine quills onto a pair of new moccasins. A group of older men sat around a low fire, exchanging stories as they chipped blades and arrowheads from the flint they had found along the beach. Several boys sat close by, listening to the tales of their elders' daring exploits. With black clay she had dug that morning at low tide, an old woman shaped a large bowl. She decorated it by pressing the fluted edge of a scallop shell into the moist clay. Behind one lodge a young girl wove a large reed basket, and not far away several men and a woman were caulking a bark canoe. The gummy substance with which they carefully covered each seam left a sweet fragrance in the damp air.

As the climbing sun at last burned through the gloomy grayness and the foggy day melted into brilliant sunshine, more villagers emerged from their homes to continue projects of sewing, weaving, and carving in the warmth of the afternoon sun.

Scenes such as this were common throughout villages of the Northeast where primitive people transformed the raw materials of their surroundings into useful articles needed for life in the forest.

Both men and women of the woodlands spent a great deal of time making things. Food preparation and garment making were tasks carried out only by the women, while the men made most of the tools and equipment needed for hunting, fishing, warfare, games, and ceremonies.

Cooking methods were similar among all the northeastern tribes, who roasted, boiled, or baked their food. In early times, cooking was done outdoors except in bad weather. Fires were built in sunken pits and much of the food was simply cooked in the flames. Most of the Woodland Indians fashioned clay pots in which they boiled food. The pot was set over the coals on stones or branches. Sometimes food such as corn was baked right in the hot ashes. When a clay pot was unavailable, kettles could be made by folding birch bark or elm bark into the shape of a container and placing the makeshift utensil on the coals. By the time the bark had been burned through the food was done. Another common cooking method, using a bark utensil, was to boil liquid in the container by adding rocks preheated in the fire. By continually replacing the hot stones, a woman kept the water boiling in the bark kettle until the food was cooked. Many nomadic northern Indians used bark utensils all the time, since they were easily made on the spot while clay pots were burdensome and breakable. In bad weather cooking had to be done inside the home where pots were often suspended over the flames on horizontal poles. In the Algonkian wigwams the poles were supported by the framework of the house.

Seneca woman pounding corn

Coastal Indians baked foods such as shellfish or a pot of beans by leaving them overnight in a covered pit in which a fire had been made. Though made famous by New Englanders, it was from the Algonkian Indians that early settlers along the coast learned about clambakes and baked beans.

Indian women used the many wild and cultivated foods of the forest to make a variety of dishes, some of which were adopted by the white man and are common foods to this day.

Corn was prepared in a number of ways. Besides being eaten on the cob, it provided the Indians with bread, soup, and foods for the trail. Roasted corn was prepared by placing the unhusked ears in the ashes of the fire and raking the hot coals over them. Sometimes the ears were supported by two small logs and roasted over the coals. Parched corn was made by browning the kernels in the fire, then pounding them into a flour with maple sugar, dried berries, or chopped meat. By adding water to the mixture a traveler could make a nourishing meal quickly and easily.

The Iroquois never added maple sugar to the parched corn when it was to be eaten by athletes or taken on the trail by hunters and warriors. It was believed that eating the sugar would make one dizzy because it came from maple trees which swayed in the wind. A corn and bean mixture, known to the coastal Indians as succotash, and a coarse gruel, which they called hominy, were foods adopted by the New England settlers and known today by the same names.

The Mohegan Indians prepared succotash by boiling beans with a lump of fat and adding green corn and scraped cobs to the mixture. Hominy was made by boiling corn with wood ashes. Lye in the ashes loosened the hulls, which were picked off and the remaining corn washed and boiled. Corn meal was made by pounding the kernels until they were a fine flour. A coarser corn meal was called "samp," from the Narragansett word *nasaump*. Both were prepared by grinding the corn in a mortar or between two stones. The meal was made into corn cakes and cooked on a flat stone or wrapped in a corn husk and baked in ashes. The addition of nuts, berries, and meat varied the taste of the corn cakes. Long ago the corn soup made by the Iroquois contained a bear's head and sometimes the head of an enemy. Modern Iroquois corn soup contains a pig's head in lieu of either of the old ingredients.

The Great Lakes Indians, with whom wild rice was a staple, ate this grain with game such as venison and duck, or they made a pudding from it. A favorite food among the Chippewa was a fish and vegetable stew containing wild rice, wild onions, dried corn, and fish. A soup eaten by the Chippewa and Pottowatomi Indians was made with wild rice and blueberries. Another soup was made from cattail roots, a plant also eaten raw, boiled, or pounded into flour for bread. Puddings were made from pumpkins and squashes or from popped corn and chestnuts. Maple sugar was added to most of these dishes as a flavoring.

Tanning hides for the making of clothing involved a number of steps before the material was ready to be worn as a garment. The tanning process was also the work of the women, who used special equipment and tools to prepare the hides.

A fresh animal skin was placed over a log which was tilted up at one end. With a scraper made from the sharpened shin bone of a deer, the tanner removed any flesh which still clung to the underside of the skin. The hide was then washed and left to soak for several days to loosen the hair. It was then put back on the log and all the hair was scraped off.

The Indians saved the brains of large animals for use in the next step of the tanning procedure. Brains cooked with fat were rubbed into the hide and it was left overnight, allowing the mixture to soak into the skin. After wringing out the hide, it was stretched on a special frame built between two close-standing trees. The whole surface was then rubbed with a stone or bone-headed tool, a laborious work which left the hide dry, soft, and white. The final step in tanning was smoking the hide and this was done by sewing the skin to form a conical bag and inverting it over a smudge fire. Smoked buckskin turned a yellow-brown to dark-brown color, depending upon the length of time it was smoked.

Tanned hides were cut and finished with as little sewing as possible. Skirts and sleeveless dresses were often draped over the body and held with a belt. When sewing was necessary, holes were first punched through the skin with a bone awl and

Tanning a hide

the thread, made from a plant fiber, was drawn through with bone or thorn needles. Even long leggings, such as the Algonkian men wore were not sewn but tied in several places along the leg. Bands worn below the knees helped to hold them up.

Sewing was required on the soft-soled moccasins worn by all the northeastern tribes. Moccasin making and design varied with each tribe, providing one distinguishing characteristic by which the different groups could be identified. A simple type of footgear was made from a single piece of hide sewed up the back and front, leaving a cuff at the ankle around which a string could be tied. A more complicated moccasin required three pieces of skin which, when sewn together formed a shoe-shape not unlike that of moccasins sold in stores today. It was a belief among the Chippewa that evil spirits lured young children to a distant land of the dead. Holes were deliberately made in a Chippewa baby's moccasins because the Indians felt that if a child had worn foot coverings the spirits would not want to take it on such a long journey.

The Woodland Indians made utensils, tools, weapons, and other equipment from materials available in their particular localities. Clay, stone, bone, shell, wood, plant fibers, and animal hides were commonly used in the making of various articles.

The northeastern tribes made pottery from clay which was powdered and mixed with shells, gravel, or sand as tempering materials. Both Algonkians and Iroquois made round-bottomed pots by the coil method, often winding ropes of clay around gourds to give their vessels rounded shapes. The gourds were left in the clay to be burned away as the pottery was fired, a process accomplished by baking the article in hot coals. The typical Iroquois pot was square-rimmed with a constricted neck and was very similar in design to pottery produced by the earlier Mound Builders. Algonkian pots were sometimes pointed at the bottom with a wide rim, while others showed the Iroquoian influence, with rounded bottoms and heavy square or rounded rims. Broken pots were mended by lacing the parts together, after which they were used as storage containers for dry food.

Various kinds of stone were used by the Indians in both worked and unworked forms. Hammerstones, pounders, grinders, and anvils often needed little work, for rocks of suitable size

Iroquois pot and pothook

and shape could easily be found. Spearheads, arrowheads, axes, adzes, gouges, drills, and scrapers were articles needing some amount of chipping, grinding, and polishing. Arrowheads were usually triangular and little over an inch in length. They were made from flint, jasper, slate, and other easily worked rocks. The spearpoint, forerunner of the arrowhead, was made from the same materials but varied more in design.

Some Ohio Indians had large flint quarries and tribes controlling supplies of the useful stone not only had raw material for their own uses but a valuable trading commodity as well. Work areas were set up near the quarries where Indian arrow makers roughed out their arrowheads and spearpoints. The flint was placed on a stone anvil and a hammerstone was used to chip off large flakes until an outline of the tool was completed. An arrowhead was notched by resting it on a sharp stone and striking an angular blow with another rock.

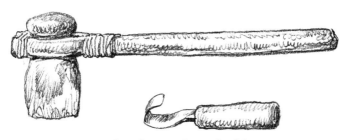

Stone hatchet and crooked knife

The stone hatchet, known also as a tomahawk, from the Algonkian word *tamahaken*, consisted of a sharpened rock attached to a wooden handle. The rock was usually grooved so that it could be securely lashed to a stick. The Eastern Cree split the handle, set the head into it, and bound the split together with deerskin thongs. Ungrooved hatchets, called *celts*, were made by wedging the stone through a hole in one end of the handle. The Iroquois used round stones set into a handle of ironwood to make fearsome war clubs. Sometimes, instead of a ball of rock, the Iroquois warrior inserted an antler spike into the end of his club. The making of axes, spears, arrows, and other weapons was a continuing task because these articles were often lost while hunting or in battles.

Bone and horn were useful materials from which the Woodland Indians fashioned blades, hooks, needles, and knife handles. Algonkians, living along the coast, made arrowpoints from the antlers of deer. A very useful tool for household tasks was the crooked knife, made by attaching a sharpened beaver's tooth to a curved handle. This knife, common to most eastern Indians, was used as the beaver had originally used its tooth for cutting— by pulling it toward the user.

Although metal was little used, native copper occurred in several eastern locations. From this, the natives hammered cylindrical beads for use as ornamentation. Evidence that they also made tools was found near New York City in the form of a copper ax. Copper objects excavated from eastern Indian mounds were made from metal gotten in trade with people of the Great Lakes region.

Shells were used as tools and utensils by most of the Indians who could obtain them and especially by the coastal Indians. Shells were in use with the earliest of these people who ate the mollusks from the sea. A variety of cups, spoons, and scrapers could be had by simply making use of the clam and mussel shells found along the beaches. Modification of certain shells, often by accident, was found to increase their usefulness, and the Indians soon learned how to break, sharpen, and drill the shells to suit specific purposes. Creatures of the sea, such as the sting ray and the horseshoe crab, provided the Indians with ready-made weapons. The Algonkians used the sharp, pointed tails of these animals to tip their spears and arrows. Weapons of war, fishing gear, farm tools, knives, axes, and tweezers were produced from shells.

Trading shells for other things resulted in their transport to the interior of the continent. Shells and articles made from shells, which were common to coastal peoples, became treasures for inland Indians. Countless articles made from shell have been found within the earthworks of the Mound Builders and many of these items are now valued in museums. Fresh-water shells were used by inland natives and also turtle shells from which cups and rattles were made.

The forest provided the Indians with an abundance of wood, bark, and plant fibers, with which they made articles for the home and the hunt. The men carved wooden pestles, bowls, cups, spoons, and ladles from different available woods. The Iroquois, who were skilled carvers, made round-bottomed cups from maple wood and decorated the handles with animal designs. The cups hung by their handles from warrior's belts when they were traveling.

The kinds of wood used by the Indians depended upon the location of the tribal territory. Some of the coastal Indians and those tribes north of the Great Lakes used birchbark extensively, but the Iroquoian tribes and Algonkians living south of the St. Lawrence River were forced to use the thicker and less desirable elm, sycamore, or hickory bark. In canoe making, bark from the large, paper birch trees made lightweight, waterproof, and durable craft which were far superior to boats made from other materials.

Construction of a birchbark canoe required several people and took as much as three weeks to complete. Women gathered spruce gum for gluing and caulking and long, thin tamarack rootlets for sewing the bark. Bark was collected in the spring and placed, inner side down, on the ground to flatten as it soaked up moisture from the earth. The wet bark was cut and fitted into shape by putting it, with the tough inner side out, into a form made of poles driven into the ground. The women glued and sewed sections of the damp bark and laced the upper edges to wooden gunwales which met at either end. Planks and ribs were added after the canoe was shaped, glued, and sewed. The canoe was then dried and all the seams caulked with a mixture of spruce gum and charcoal which had been fried in grease. It was this substance which made dark seams on the canoes.

The canoe makers of the Northeast were highly skilled in their work, a fact noted by George Waymouth, who described the boats he saw as he explored Maine and northern Massachusetts in 1605. "Their canoes are made of bark strengthened within

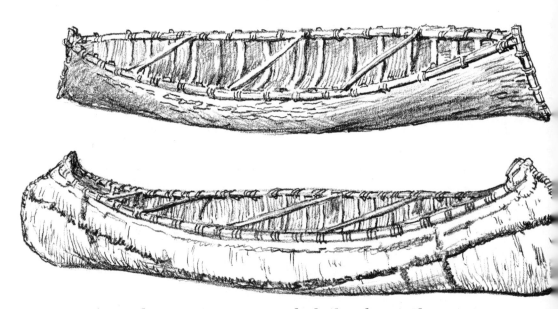

Above: Iroquois canoe of elm bark. Below: A Chippewa birchbark canoe.

with ribs and hoops of wood, in so good fashion and with such excellent ingenious art, as our men that had been often in the Indies, said they far exceeded any that ever they had seen."

Indians, in whose lands the big birch trees did not grow, made dugout canoes from large logs. This involved felling a suitable tree, obtaining a length of it, removing the bark, and hollowing out the log's interior. Except for removal of the bark, the entire process had to be done by burning the wood and scraping away at the charcoal with stone adzes or shell scrapers.

Birchbark was also an excellent material for making containers. The Indians of the North made trays from birchbark squares which they cut and folded up at the corners. Deeper containers, called *makuks*, were made in much the same way but had seams

Penobscots building a canoe

up the sides and a wooden rim around the top for reinforcement.

Another article made of wood and leather by both Algonkians and Iroquois was the cradleboard to which mothers strapped their infants from birth until the child could walk. The carrier was made of a flat board with a footboard at the bottom and a bow at the top which protected the baby's face. A burden strap made of leather passed around the mother's forehead or shoulders when she carried the child. The strap could also be used to hang the cradleboard from a peg in the home or outside.

Containers, mats, and ropes were made from bark fibers, grasses, and reeds by braiding and weaving. Cedar bark, rushes, cornhusks, and cattails were woven into mats or made into storage bags. Those tribes with birchbark supplies did not need to weave baskets and bags, since containers of bark were so much easier to make. The Iroquois used elm bark to make containers such as storage barrels, maple sap tubs, trays, and bowls. Woven from the inner fibers of the elm, basswood, and cedar were burden straps, also called *tumplines*. These were bands, most often worn around the forehead, which had ties at the ends so that women could carry baskets, babies, and other burdens on their backs. They were also used by men to support wooden pack frames used on long trips.

In a country of snowy winters, hunting gear included snowshoes. Snowshoes date back to at least 4000 B.C. when an unknown Asian craftsman made the first pair. The invention spread to North America in the form of long, flat boards like skis. Among the tribes of the Northeast the design was varied—some being oval, while others were racket-shaped. The Iroquois made snowshoes with a hickory frame, two crossbars, and a hexagonal netting of skin thongs. Rawhide straps fastened the snowshoe to the foot. Women wore shorter, rounder snowshoes than the men. Algonkian snowshoes looked much like those of the Iroquois, but were made with an ash frame, cut green, and bent

A tumpline in use

to shape over a fire. Besides snowshoes, the Indians made wooden toboggans, for use in carrying equipment and the animals they killed.

A wood craft learned by Indians from boyhood was bow and arrow making. Bows varied with the different tribes, but the eastern Indians preferred to make them from one length of springy wood such as shagbark hickory, white ash, cedar, or white oak.

A wooden weapon made in the woodlands only by the Iroquoian people was a blowgun. This was a tube used with darts to kill small animals. The blowgun was a shaft, up to six feet long, which had been split, hollowed out, and glued back together.

Wampum making was a laborious task carried on mainly by coastal Algonkians. "Wampum" is a word derived from an Algonkian term *wampumpeag* which means "white strings" and refers to strings of cylindrical shell beads. Wampum served many purposes among the Indians of the Northeast prior to the white man's use of it for money. Woodland peoples used the wampum for decorations, gift giving, treaty ratification, and conveyance of messages. A very important commodity among the Iroquois, it was called *otekoa*, the name of a fresh-water shell from which their earliest beads were made. Although highly valued by the Iroquois, few beads were ever manufactured by these tribes. The powerful Iroquois received wampum from weaker tribes in trade, as tribute, or from raids. The wampum was valuable because of the difficulty involved in producing the beads. Algonkian craftsmen used quahog and periwinkle shells, which they cut, polished, and drilled, to make the purple and white beads. Boring the lengthwise hole in the shell was done with stone or wooden drills in wet sand and was a tedious job since the beads were only about one-eighth inch in diameter and up to one-half inch long. Wampum belts several feet to several yards in length were woven by the Iroquois, using animal sinews or plant fibers to hold the beads.

Most dance ceremonies of the Woodland Indians were accompanied by instrumental music and singing. The Indians produced drums, rattles, rhythm sticks, and a kind of flute. The materials used in the making of these instruments were important because they represented plants and animals important in Indian life.

The Iroquois made a water drum from a small hollowed-out

A Naskapi on snowshoes

log or from folded bark. This was fitted with a watertight bottom and over the top was stretched a piece of rawhide. The drum could be partly filled with water through a hole in the side.

Depending upon the water level, different tones were produced.

Rattles were made from bark, horns, gourds, and turtle shells. The turtle-shell rattles were significant among the Iroquois because these Indians believed that the whole earth grew on the back of a great turtle.

A wind instrument which the Iroquois are often credited with inventing is the flageolet. This is a flutelike instrument made from red cedar, having six finger holes with which different tones are produced. The flageolet is not used in ceremonies but only for pleasure, and some experts believe that the Indians adopted it from the Europeans.

The Woodland Indian used materials from the forest and the sea to create works of art. Sometimes his art took the form of ornaments or decorations on clothing, tools, weapons, and utensils. The Indian sculptor created animals of wood and stone, and pipes of clay. The ancient Mound Builders carved thousands of stone pipes and made gigantic effigy mounds in the shapes of animals and birds. Iroquois mask makers cut grotesque faces from living trees. Most of the forest people made pictographs on bark, skin, and stone, or wove them on sashes.

The artwork of the Indian was more than decorative and for him the use of certain materials, designs, and colors had deep religious meaning or was otherwise symbolic.

Decorative arts were similar among the many Woodland tribes, probably due to the years of close association in which the cultures gradually blended. The earliest pre-European designs of the Iroquois have been preserved on their pottery. These were groups of incised parallel lines arranged in angular combinations. Later designs took the form of symmetrical curves much like those of the Algonkians, and it is believed that the Iroquois adopted this art form after migrating into Algonkian lands. A similar and very common motif used by both Algonkians and Iroquois was the double curve, which was at first embroidered with moose hair or porcupine quills on clothing and bags. The Indians also used plant fibers and beads of stone, shell, bone, and fired clay in making the embroidered designs. More recent are the complicated but non-symbolic floral designs using glass beads obtained from the white man. The earlier curved line designs with which the Indians decorated much of their clothing were symbolic of various natural phenomena, peace, health, and political organization. The scrolls used in decorating the borders of leggings, skirts, and moccasin flaps had political meaning because they represented the horns of chieftaincy and are known as "horned" trimmings. A circle, one of the oldest figures used by the Woodland Indians, was the symbol for life. Animal designs represented various clans and totems.

Colors were also symbolic, and dyes obtained from roots, husks, and seeds were used by the women to color quills, plant fibers, leather, and wood.

The use of symbolic colors and designs was of great importance in Indian communication and in the custom of using wampum belts for political purposes.

Chapter 7

━━━━◆◆◆━━━━

CUSTOMS AND COMMUNICATION

AN IROQUOIS WARRIOR was walking alone in a thick forest when he heard a strange sound. As he peered cautiously through the leaves he saw a large bird which, instead of being clad in feathers, was covered with wampum. The warrior knew that this was a spirit bird which had become lost. He quietly retraced his steps back to the village and told the head chief what he had seen. The chief called a great council meeting to tell all the warriors that the one among them who could bring back the wampum bird would win the chief's daughter for his own.

The warriors quickly made their way into the dense woods and found the great bird perched atop the tallest tree in the forest. Many arrows were spent and some of them hit the bird, causing strings of wampum to fall to the ground. A few warriors were satisfied to pick up the fallen treasure and run home. When they reached the village their wealth had turned to turkey feathers and the crestfallen men hid themselves in their houses.

The remaining warriors shot many arrows at the wampum bird, but it neither flew away nor did it fall from its perch. A young boy from another village came to watch the efforts of the warriors. When none of the marksmen met with success the child asked if he too might shoot at the bird. The request was granted and the astonished warriors watched while, with one shot, the boy killed the magnificent bird and presented the fallen prize to the chief.

The boy was married to the chief's daughter and became a chief himself. He decreed that the wampum be divided between his own tribe and the one into which he had married. A law was made that from that time on wampum should be the price of peace and blood. When war was declared on any tribe a belt of wampum was sent to the enemy and when the war was over wampum was exchanged as a token of peace.

Some tribes believe this ancient legend explains how wampum came to be used symbolically in peace and war.

The use of wampum was an important custom among many of the northeastern tribes. The drilled beads were sometimes used as ornamentation, but the wampum which was woven into belts took on a greater importance to the Indians. The woven belts contained symbolic patterns formed by the arrangement of the white and purple wampum beads. The pictorial representations of the wampum belts became a means of recording events, sending messages, and binding agreements. The use of wampum as a pictographic device for aiding the memory probably began when the beads were given as gifts and the recipients wished to keep them in remembrance of the event. The belts could be interpreted because a particular design was associated with a particular idea. The tribes of the Iroquois Confederacy used wampum in all their political agreements and the belts became public records which were kept by an Onondaga sachem who was called the Keeper of the Wampum. It was the duty of this appointed chief to know the meanings of the symbols on the belts and to interpret them when they were displayed. Wampum belts commemorated treaties made by the Indians, both among themselves and with white men. Usually, when an agreement was made between two parties, duplicate belts were woven and each kept one. The holders of the various belts told their stories at ceremonies and among themselves to insure that the meanings were not forgotten.

Several famous belts are still in existence, including the Hiawatha Belt. This, the oldest known belt, recorded the formation of the Iroquois League. The Washington Covenant Belt represents the peace agreement between the thirteen colonies and the Six Nations of the Iroquois. (At the time of the agreement the Tuscaroras had been admitted to the Confederacy.) The William Penn Belt, which was woven of nearly 3,000 beads, was given to the famous founder of Pennsylvania in 1682 in commemoration of a treaty. It shows an Indian grasping the hand of a white man in friendship. One man is wearing a hat, showing him to be a European.

The colors used were as important as the design in giving meaning to the belts. White beads indicated purity, faith, and peace, while black threatened war. Beads covered with clay showed grief. A black belt with the sign of a hatchet painted on it in red was a war belt. It could be sent to another tribe with tobacco as an invitation to join in war. The belts served as passports to couriers who traveled from tribe to tribe. In summoning council meetings the chiefs were given message belts and when they appeared at a general meeting the wampum served as their credentials. To help prevent a wampum shortage it was the custom that for the gift of a belt an equal amount of wampum was expected in return. Belts which represented broken treaties or unimportant transactions and events were unstrung and the beads reused.

Wampum had great power among the Indians. It is said that Logan, a famous Iroquois chief, once saved a white captive from Indian torturers by rushing in among them and throwing a wampum strip about the prisoner's neck. The man was then freed in Logan's custody.

The early Indians did not use wampum as money except in one instance. A murderer could pay off the relatives of his victim with six strings of wampum if it was agreeable to everyone. If not, the relatives had the right to slaughter their kinsman's killer.

The Europeans found that wampum was a good substitute for the hard-to-get coins from the Old World, and the beads gained a monetary value. King Philip, a Wampanoag chief, is supposed to have worn a coat made of wampum from which he cut pieces whenever he was in need of money.

Pictographs served many purposes among the Woodland people. Some of them, such as the designs on wampum belts, commemorated great events, while others scratched on bark or incised on rocks were messages, notices, and reminders of songs, dances, ceremonies, and events. Other pictographs were connected with religion and mythology.

Among the Chippewa, the word *kekeewin* meant pictographs which could be understood by most tribal members, but *kekeenowin* referred to things known only to the priests, prophets, and other mystery men of their tribe. The word Ojibwa, the true name of the Chippewa Indians, is translated to mean "those who make pictographs."

Throughout the Northeast, lasting examples of Indian picture writing have been found in the form of rock carvings called petroglyphs. Other pictographs were made upon bone, wood, bark, shell, hide, and human skin. The latter were in the form of tattoos. All symbols made by persons of a particular tribe were identical. A picture made upon bark and fastened to a tree could tell a warrior's tribesmen that enemies had passed by, who they were, how many there were, and in which direction they were headed. Among the Abenaki, cutting the bark from a tree on one, two, or three sides indicated that a person had had poor, poorer, or poorest luck. Cutting all around the tree meant "I am starving." The Ottawa and Pottowatomi indicated starvation by drawing a black line across the breast or stomach of a pictured person.

One symbol made by the Chippewa Indians, combining a bird and a man, has been found to be identical to a pictographic character common to the people of Siberia. This is perhaps an indication of the origin and the antiquity of Indian picture writing.

The Delaware or Lenni Lenape Indians are known for a very

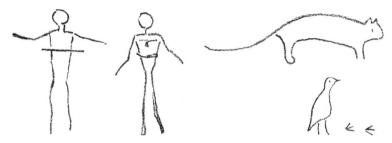

Pictographs: Left, symbols for starvation. Right, symbols for panther, turkey, and turkey tracks.

famous pictographic record called the Walum-Olum, or Red Record. It was originally a number of notched sticks, each about six inches long. A picture was painted in the notch of each stick to represent a great event in the history of the tribe. Copies of 184 of these pictures were preserved and tell a story of the creation of the world and the tribal history of the Lenni Lenape. The meanings of the painted notches were taught by the older chiefs to the younger tribesmen and in this way the story was perpetuated. Part of the Walum-Olum tells how the Lenni Lenape came from the Northwest and crossed the Namesi Sipu, or "river of fish," into the country of the Great Serpent. This has been interpreted as the crossing of the Mississippi River into the lands of the Mound Builders. The migrants may have come upon the huge earthen serpent built by the Mound Builders which exists today in southern Ohio. The last marks on the sticks are supposed to mean "The white men have come from the north and the south. They are peaceful; they have great things. Who are they?"

Pictographs were but one aid to the memory in cultures where the use of words was unknown in recording ideas. Among the Sac and Fox there was a very long legend about their great teacher, Wisuka. In order to remember every part of the story the singers or reciters used a "micam." This was a wooden box in which various objects were kept. Each object was a reminder to the storyteller of a part of the story, and by using the micam he could be sure that no part of the tale was omitted.

Among the customs of the northeastern Indians was the practice of holding regular festivals throughout the year. These festivals were great social occasions and, though joyous in nature, the rituals performed were very serious. Those tribes for whom agriculture was a way of life based their festivals on the growing of crops.

The Iroquois held eight public festivals annually and some modern Iroquois people have continued the custom. A New Year festival was held at the first new moon of the new year and it lasted about three weeks. There was much speechmaking and the confession of sins. A sincere confession was one made while holding white wampum. Following the confessions a dance of peace known as Ustuaguna was done, feasts and games were held, and the medicine men dispelled witches and disease. A part of this festival was the White Dog ceremony in which the purest-colored dog to be found was killed and roasted. The Indians believed that they were sending the animal to the skies as a messenger.

In a festival connected with the annual tapping of the maple

Sac and Fox storyteller using a micam box

trees, the war dance was performed to bring on warmer weather and the free flowing of sap. A feast was also held at the end of the maple sugaring season. Three festivals were related to the growing of corn—one at the time of planting, another when the green ears appeared, and the third at harvest time. A strawberry and a bean festival made up the remaining feasts. In addition to these eight public festivals many other less important feasts were held during the year.

The Algonkians began to hold festivals after they had become more agricultural and lived in larger groupings than just family units. Feasts were held when tribes moved from their summer places to winter homes. Their festivals included the telling and enactment of stories and myths.

Unlike the Iroquoian tribes, where descent was traced through the mother and women had a good deal of importance, the Algonkians based descent on the father's family. Marriage was often merely a consent of two people to become man and wife. A marriage could be ended as simply as it was begun. The Naskapis could take more than one wife and a good hunter often did so, for he needed more than one woman to keep up with the work. Women were considered inferior and while Naskapi boys were given every advantage, baby girls were neglected. The Wyandots allowed a man to have more than one wife as long as each wife was from a different clan.

Many customs and superstitions were associated with naming an individual. It was usual for an Indian baby to be named according to a clan. Later, new names were given as a result of deeds and adventures. Most Indians had several names, including uncomplimentary ones. Some tribes never mentioned a child's name again after it was first given, since it was feared that anyone knowing the name would be able to do harm to the person. In order to prevent witchcraft another name was substituted for the original one.

A name usually had pictographic possibilities so that the person could be easily represented in a drawing. As examples, the Iroquois names, Large Mouth (Hosahoho), Long Feather (Sahawhe), Growing Flower (Aweont), and the Chippewa names, Little Star (Anougons) and It Begins to Dawn (Bidaban), are all pictographic. The Indians even renamed white men with whom they dealt so that these people could be identified in pictures. William Penn was given the name Onas, which in Mohawk meant "feather quill."

Indians disciplined their children little and rarely if ever struck their offspring. The Kickapoo of Illinois enjoyed a plan in which naughty children might be punished and their parents spared the unhappiness of spanking them. The Kickapoo had a tribe whipper who circulated the camps weekly and whipped any child who had misbehaved during the preceding week.

The Iroquois had few discipline problems, for their children were told of "Long Nose," a terrible cannibal who went about kidnapping youngsters who misbehaved and carried them off in a great pack basket.

To the Indian, death meant passing into the spirit world, which was nearby and similar to the world of the living. Spirits were considered more powerful than living persons and people sometimes feared the ghosts of the dead. Houses of dead persons were often burned and the relatives disfigured themselves so that they would not be recognized by the spirit of the deceased.

Burials were in trees, on scaffolds, and in the ground, either in mounds or underground graves. With the dead warrior were placed his prized possessions—weapons, utensils, and ornaments —all the things he would need in his new life after death.

The Chippewa Indians marked the grave of a departed tribesman with a post upon which a totem symbol was carved to tell the person's clan name. Other marks were placed on the grave post to record battles or other events in which the person had participated.

The Hurons buried their dead in bark coffins which were raised on a scaffold. Gifts of food, weapons, and other articles were left by the mourners at the burial site. About every twelve years a Feast of the Dead was held and the bodies or bones of all who had died within that time were collected, rewrapped, and buried in a common pit. To insure that the deceased were not forgotten, their names were given to others. Anyone receiv-

ing the name of an outstanding person was expected to live up
to that name by performing a courageous feat.

The Iroquois buried their dead in the ground and sometimes
erected mounds over the bodies. Usually a large, round hole was
excavated and the body placed upright in it. The grave was covered with timber to keep the earth from falling in upon the body.

In 1838, Black Hawk, the famous Sac warrior, was buried according to tribal tradition, in a seated position on the ground
under a wooden shelter.

The Northern Cree gave notice of death by hanging an object
which represented the deceased upon a tree in the path of any-

Huron burial

one returning to the village. Persons coming into the village were in this way warned against mentioning the name of the dead person.

Mourning was carried on in many ways. Among the Hurons mourning lasted for a year and after a death close relatives spent at least ten days lying face down on a mat and speaking to almost no one. The Sac showed their grief by rubbing charcoal on their faces, fasting, and slashing their arms and legs. They believed that by cutting themselves they could let out their internal grief.

The Indians of the Northeast played many games. Their sports were for enjoyment and also for religious purposes, as they believed that by playing games they pleased the spirits. Sometimes during famines or epidemics games were played as part of the ceremonies to appease the spirits.

One of the games played by many Indian tribes throughout the continent and the national game of the northeastern tribes was lacrosse. This sport, popular today, got its name from the racket used to play the game. The French likened the implement to a bishop's crozier and called it "la crosse" which soon became the word lacrosse. The Iroquois played the game for fun and also as useful training for war. Any tactics were allowed in the game as the teams of trained warriors attempted to make goals. Each player had a racket with which he caught and threw a ball made from a knot of wood. Often the rackets were used as clubs and players ended up with broken limbs and cracked heads. The game was played on a large field or on ice in the winter. Gates which were used as goals were placed at either end of the field about sixty yards apart. Teams consisted of six to eight men who played from noon until evening and often concluded a game the following day. Intertribal games were held on field days set aside for games.

Though lacrosse was a common game, it was only played by

the men but there were ball games played only among women too. One of these, known as double ball, was a team sport in which each player used a curved stick to toss and catch the balls. Balls were sand-filled buckskin bags tied with a long leather thong. Players tossed the balls to one another in an attempt to make goals.

Shinny was another women's sport, somewhat like hockey, in which curved sticks were used to hit a flattened buckskin ball and get it through goal posts at the ends of the field.

Variations of a hoop game were played by teams, with the object being to get sticks, poles, or spears through a rolling hoop. The team which got the most spears through the hoop was the winner. Sometimes the objective was to stop a rolling hoop by impaling it with a spear.

A popular winter sport among all the northern tribes was snow snake, a game played with smooth, flexible, maple sticks from five to nine feet long. The making of the tapered rod which was called a snow snake was an art, and good snow snakes were cherished by their owners. The head of the stick curved up and was carved like a serpent's head. The object of the game was to throw the snow snake, which was rubbed with a secret oil, the farthest distance in the shortest time along a specially prepared track. The track was a hollowed trough in the snow which was packed smooth and watered to make an icy surface.

Target shooting was a game in which the players used specially marked arrows and bows that took exceptional strength to pull. Another popular game was throwing the arrow, in which the player tried to throw as many arrows into the air as he could before the first one hit the ground.

Many tribes played a game using several moccasins or other containers into which objects such as bones, pits, or buttons were placed. These items were identical except for one which was inconspicuously marked. The opposing team tried to guess the

The snow snake game

moccasin into which the marked object had been placed. Tallies
were kept by using pieces of wood made for that purpose.

Gambling was a favorite pastime of the Woodland Indians and
games of chance were especially enjoyed during the winter when
outdoor sports were limited. Many kinds of dice games were
played with bone or horn buttons or peach stones. The dice
were usually painted on one side and placed in a bowl which
was struck, causing the dice to fly out. The rules assigned a number of counters to particular dice-throw combinations. Beans
were often used as counters and the player or team which won

The scalp lock of the Iroquois

all the beans won the game. Stakes included such things as blankets, furs, pipes, wives, and even fingers. When a finger was bet and lost, the winner customarily took it to wear on a necklace.

An Iroquois myth about the good and evil twins tells how the good twin played a game of Bowl and Counters with his evildoing grandmother to see which twin would rule the world. Fortunately, the good twin was clever enough to defeat his grandmother. At two of their festivals the Iroquois played the great gambling game of Peach Stones and Bowl in remembrance of the good twin's victory.

Various customs were connected with hunting and fishing. The Hurons never threw the bones of a fish into the fire, for they believed that the spirit of the fish would then warn the other fish against being caught. The Hurons also believed that their fishing nets could see, hear, eat, and talk to the fish. For this reason they had a fish preacher who addressed the fish in an attempt to lure them into the nets.

Scalping was not a prevalent practice among tribes other than the Iroquois, who wore the famous scalp locks. It was not a custom in New England until the white man began paying bounties for the scalps of certain Indians and even of other white men.

As with most primitive people, the Indian observed his world and from his observations formulated methods for telling time. He measured days by the rising and setting of the sun and recorded the passage of months by the waxing and waning of the moon. He correlated seasons with the cycles of animals and plants of the forest. He attributed seasonal changes to the acts of his gods and made deities of the winds which brought warmth and moisture or ice and snow. The Iroquois believed the seasons were brought about by a constant struggle between a good and evil spirit.

Many eastern tribes divided the year into five parts, corresponding to natural events. To these Indians there was a spring, a time of corn ripening, a high sun time or summer, a leaf falling time, and winter.

The Chippewa named the months for natural phenomena and called them moons. September was the Ripe-rice Moon and October the Harvest Moon. November was the Moon of Menabozho, whom the Chippewa credited with bringing a second summer each year. (Today this time of year is known as Indian Summer.) December was the Moon of the Dropping Horns because at this time the deer shed its antlers.

The Iroquois watched the Northern Lights and attributed different meanings to the heavenly hues. When their dominant color was yellow the Indians believed that there would be

A Cayuga orator

trouble in the Nation. Red skies stood for bloodshed, but mottled heavens in the spring was a good sign and the Iroquois danced to please the spirits who might give them a good growing season.

Having no true written language, the Indians carried on much of their communication orally. Besides native storytellers who kept alive and enriched the tribal folklore, there were also talented orators among the Indians. After the arrival of the Europeans many Indian orators achieved a lasting prominence in

American history. Eloquence was thought of by the Indian as second only to courage, and orators were respected and admired by their tribesmen as well as by the white men. Indian oratory was slow, deliberate, and repetitious, but very logical and dignified. Iroquois orators gave wampum belts as they spoke, to verify their statements.

Many Indian orators became famous for speeches given in defense of themselves and their race. Among the best remembered Indian orators are Logan and Red Jacket. Red Jacket, probably the greatest orator ever produced by the Indians, was said to have shown a timidity in battle which would have disgraced him had it not been for his eloquence. Red Jacket thrilled even his enemies with his oratorical genius.

On cold evenings the Indians sat about their fires listening to the tales of a storyteller. The telling of tribal myths and legends was done both as a form of instruction and for entertainment. As years passed and contact with the white man grew, Indian stories began to change and incorporate ideas from the newcomers. Some of the stories of the northern coastal Indians tell of a wolf, as in legends of the Norsemen, while other native legends include the Christian concepts of a savior and a Great Spirit. The stories which were least affected by white contact were those of the Chippewa and other tribes not directly in the path of European expansion.

Chippewa storytellers taught their children about Menabozho, their culture hero, and Iagoo, a legendary storyteller who was believed to have first told the tales to their ancestors.

Chapter 8

————◆◆————

RELIGION, MYTHOLOGY, AND FOLKLORE

BEFORE BEDTIME on frosty nights the Chippewa children gathered about the winking fire and listened to the stories that grandfather told. Sometimes the white-haired old man told them of Iagoo, the great storyteller who had visited the lodge of his forefathers. This night grandfather told one of the many legends Iagoo had related about the hero, Menabozho.

He said, "My grandfather told me of Menabozho, who was very powerful but was once outwitted by a small boy. The boy dared the great Manitou to do as he did. The boy put his great toe into his mouth. Menabozho tried to do this but found he could not. He told the boy he need but make a wish and it would come true. The boy thought, then wished for a long life, and Menabozho instantly changed him into a tall white cedar tree. For hundreds of winters the tree stood rooted on the very spot where Menabozho had fulfilled the boy's wish. This was the cruel reward the great Menabozho gave the boy for outwitting him. To be wiser than a Manitou is not a good thing."

When grandfather had ended his nightly story the children climbed under their soft deerskin robes to go to sleep. Their mother told them that soon Weenk was coming with his tiny warriors to conquer their eyelids. The children could almost feel the tiny Weenk and his little braves landing, for their eyes would not stay open. Weenk and his men made their eyelids very heavy, and shortly the Chippewa children were fast asleep.

The Indians of the woodlands practiced a religion which influenced every facet of their lives. It was a practical religion which dealt with their immediate needs, yet it was a religion filled with superstition, supernatural beings, and hierarchies of gods. If he was troubled, the Indian made offerings to the spirits and in this way sought to relieve his problems. He was careful to appease both the good and the evil spirits. The early missionaries interpreted his offerings to evil spirits as worship of the Devil. An evil spirit, to the Indian, was one which brought him misfortune, such as the North Wind, bringer of ice and snow and killer of his food crops, but this was only one among many spirits in the Indian's world.

The forest people believed in an impersonal force which permeated all of nature and in that way influenced their destiny. This great power which filled the sky and the world was called Manitou by Algonkians and Orenda by the Iroquois. The white man likened this force to their own God, and the term "Great Spirit" came into being. Manitou and Orenda were, however, made up of many spirits inhabiting every object in the Indian's world. The Indian believed in a life after death in which he was a spirit living a life much like his earthly one. He did not believe that his soul or shadow was punished for earthly deeds, but rather than it retained the human needs for sleeping, eating, and hunting. The Iroquois believed that warrior spirits lived in the sky and other ancestral spirits lived in an underworld with a Mother of Animals. This underworld was a beautiful place where there was no war, hunger, or disease.

To fill the gaps in his knowledge of the world and of himself

Weenk and his tiny warriors

were the Indian myths, telling of gods, supernatural beings, and natural phenomena. There were tales of tribal traditions, wars, and legendary heroes. The Indians told fairy tales and fables about giants, pygmies, witches, and animals. The myths and tales of the Woodland peoples made up a rich folklore through which their beliefs were strengthened and perpetuated.

Early Algonkian hunters had a simple religion in which the spirits of the hunt and of their ancestors were primary. The animal world was one with the world of men and the early hunters were as close to the spirit world as to their families. These people believed that all the animals could speak. The Naskapi thought that the Canada jay informed other animals of the hunter's approach and it was for this reason that they often killed the talkative bird. As contacts with other people increased and agriculture was adopted, the Algonkian's religion became a blend of the primitive hunting beliefs and a mythology related to agriculture. The newer religion retained the ancestor worship and incorporated spirits of fertility, seasons, winds, and stars.

The Iroquois, whose society was more complex and dependent primarily upon agriculture, had a religion incorporating imaginative mythology about nature. The oldest Iroquois deities are the animals, which were said to have been transformed into humans and from whom the various clans grew, such as the turtle who became a man and began the Turtle Clan.

One of the foremost Iroquois gods was Hinu, the Thunder God. To gain the favor of this mighty spirit the Indians burned tobacco whenever Hinu approached the earth. This god was given credit for ridding the earth of giant animals, as the Indians sometimes found the bones of the huge prehistoric creatures which had once roamed their lands. Hinu was a kindly god and punished only those who offended him. A Seneca legend tells of his goodness and the creation of Niagara's horsehoe-shaped falls.

A lovely maiden had been promised in marriage to a hideous old war chief. The young girl could not bear to become the wife

The god Hinu

of the ugly old man and paddled her canoe to the edge of great Niagara Falls, preferring to die in the roaring waters than to marry the chief. The great god Hinu, who lived behind the falls and watched over the harvests, saw the maiden falling to her death and caught her before she was dashed on the rocks. Hinu kept the girl in his cave for a long time and taught her many things. She learned that many of her people were sick and dying because a snake lay coiled beneath the ground upon which her village stood. This evil serpent crept about, poisoning the waters because he craved human flesh and could not be satisfied by the small number of people who died naturally.

One day, when Hinu came back from looking over the crops, he told the girl that she might now return to her people, for her unwanted suitor was dead. The maiden went to her people and told them of Hinu and the evil spirit beneath the village. The tribe moved its village many times, but the clever serpent followed and sickness continued. Hinu came to the aid of the people by finding the evil snake and hurling giant thunderbolts at it until it was dead. The body of the dead serpent was so large that as it floated down the waters of Niagara it became wedged in the rocks and its tremendous weight pressed down the rocks, fashioning a giant horseshoe which still can be seen today. The good god Hinu had ended the sickness which plagued the village.

Another beneficent god was the West Wind, Hinu's brother, who helped the great Thunder God bring rain for the Iroquois crops. The North Wind, Ka-tash-huaht, was feared by the people because he brought death. A story tells that Hinu chased the howling Ka-tash-huaht far to the North where he rants and raves to this day and punishes those who come too near his icy abode.

The Iroquois had a special god called Goweh, the god of war. Goweh only answered to the call of the Iroquois and was known also as the Echo God. Before going to war the Iroquois called upon Goweh, and if they did not receive an answer they postponed their attack until the deity called back to them. The Holder of the Heavens, Tarhuhyiawahku, is known for bringing forth the six tribes of the Iroquois from the island of Mother Earth.

Besides the great gods, there were spirits such as the sisters who watched over the vegetables, and Tsentsa and Taweskare, the good and evil twin sons of the West Wind, who shaped the earth. The Iroquois believed that supernatural beings existed in the form of Great Heads and cannibal giants. There were witches, pygmies, and demigods, such as Hiawatha and the wizard Todadaho with his hair of writhing serpents.

The Great Heads were bodiless creatures with long streaming hair and huge eyes. They were ever watchful and their hair helped them to fly about on errands both merciful and destructive. It is said that one of these monsters appeared at the door of an old woman's home one night as she sat by her fire parching corn. Believing that the woman was actually eating live coals from the fire, the bodiless creature was frightened away and none of its kind were ever seen again.

The Stone Giants were huge beings who came from the West to kill the eastern Indians. An old story tells of a group of Seneca warriors who accepted a challenge to battle some of the giants near a great gulf. When the time came for the encounter a mighty wind from the West blew the Stone Giants into the water and they were never able to get out. The West Wind became highly revered among the Seneca.

The pygmies were tiny little people who were responsible for carving the rocks into strange shapes and creating cliffs and caves. They also had ways to destroy monsters. There are many stories telling how these friendly little forest elves helped their Indian neighbors.

The Chippewa called these little people *pukwudjinnies* and one of their tales tells how the pukwudjinnies conquered a wicked giant, or *weedigo*. Kwasind was an evil weedigo and very strong, but he was foolish and told the little water people called *nibanabas* that he could be hurt if he was hit on the back of his head. The nibanabas told the secret to the pukwudjinnies who resolved to rid the forest of this giant. They gathered pine cones and waited until the enormous Kwasind had been lulled to sleep in his great canoe by the singing of the little water people. They crept up to where the slumbering giant lay face down and threw the pine cones into his canoe. Some of the cones struck Kwasind on the back of his head and his wickedness was ended forever.

The Algonkians believed that manitous inhabited everything on earth and in space. The manitous' powers were of different degrees. The superior manitou among the Chippewa was called Kitshi Manitou. Kitshi, or Kechi, is an Algonkian word for chief. Another Chippewa manitou was the Ghost Spirit who ruled the "place of shadows," the hereafter. The Abenaki believed they were created by their good god, Kechi Niwaski, who modeled their ancestors in the form of wooden Indians. They believed that the god first shaped them from stone but, being dissatisfied with his handiwork, he then made a perfect pair from wood.

Probably the most famous Algonkian manitou was known as Menabozho. This great culture hero is known by many names among the different tribes, including Nanabojo, Winabojo, Nana-bush, and Missaba. Menabozho is translated to mean the Great White Hare. Other interpretations give its meaning as "god of light" or "ruler of the sun." Most people know of Menabozho under the name of Hiawatha, whose adventures were told by Longfellow in his *Song of Hiawatha*. Longfellow merely substituted the name Hiawatha for the Chippewa name of the legendary hero.

Menabozho could take many forms and he had many homes.

He often appeared on earth as a man. Some stories say he lived in the East and ruled the sun. Without the manitou, the sun could not make its daily journey across the sky. Others say that

A Great Head

Menabozho lived on an ice mountain. He was a brother to all creatures and plants, and could step over mountains and lakes with ease. It is said that when the sun hides each night it is Menabozho resting. He was called the Trickster and the Sly One

135

because he sometimes used cunning to get his way. Menabozho is supposed to have acted as an intermediary between Kitshi Manitou and the Chippewa Indians. Some people think that the Indians believed it was Menabozho coming when the white man first appeared in their lands.

The Cree Indians tell of another Trickster, Wisagatcak, who created the earth. Part of the story tells how, when the earth was flooded, Wisagatcak built a raft and collected various animals, including a raven which flew over the water in a vain search for land. The story is similar to that of Noah and the Ark except that Wisagatcak solved his problem magically by calling on the wolf, who ran around the raft with a clump of moss in his mouth. The moss grew until it covered the raft and made the world.

Other Algonkian peoples have a myth somewhat like the Iroquois story of the good and evil brothers. The Algonkian's creator force was called Gluskap and his brother was Malsum. Among Penobscot Indians, Gluskap was spelled Kluskabe, while the Passamaquoddys knew him as Kuloscap or Glooscap. Gluskap's brother Malsum made all the evil things and Gluskap killed him, driving his bad magic underground. There Malsum became a cruel wolf, in the manner of Norse mythology. Like Menabozho, Gluskap, the wonder worker, had all sorts of adventures and was eventually defeated by his pride. He is supposed to have left the land in a birchbark canoe and traveled to the sunshine. The Indians believed he would someday return.

The Indians had firm beliefs in witchcraft, carnivorous ghosts, and the awesome power of priests and sorcerers. They believed that a person's body could be in one place and his spirit elsewhere, and that some persons could take animal shapes. The Algonkians had priests called shamans who through their own magic could make journeys to visit the "old people" or spirits of the ancestors in the underworld. By inducing a trance, a shaman could visit the land of spirits, but he must not accept

Menabozho

food from them, for if he did so his spirit would be captured and his entranced body on earth would die. It was the reports of these shamans which convinced the Indians that there was an afterlife.

Among the Chippewa and many other associated tribes of Algonkian peoples, including the Ottawa, Pottowatomi, Sac, Fox, Miami, and others, there was a society known as the Grand Medicine Society. Among the Chippewa this organization for shamans was called the Midewiwin. To train as a Mide or member of the Society, candidates paid fees consisting of robes, furs, blankets, tobacco, or other articles of value. There were four levels within the Midewiwin and members were promoted for fees which grew successively larger at each step. Few members ever reached the fourth level, as the price was extremely high. The Mide went through extensive study, prior to initiation, in which he or she learned the medicinal plants, how to cure diseases or ailments, and to communicate with manitous. Initiates were purified in a sweat lodge and inducted in a specially built lodge called a Midewigan or "Grand Medicine Lodge." According to tradition, it was Menabozho who gave the secrets of the Midewiwin to the Chippewa people. It was believed that Menabozho was present in the Grand Medicine Lodge of the Society. The second most powerful manitou under Kitshi Manitou was called Dzhe Manitou, or the Good Spirit, and he was the guardian of the Midewiwin.

Priests of the Midewiwin preserved the Society's traditions by keeping birchbark records. These were seen only by members of the Midewiwin. Women could join the Society but were restricted to the treatment of women and children and the curing of headaches, toothaches, and neuralgia by means of tatoos. Tatoos were made by pricking the skin with a needle-like instrument directly on the affected area in order to drive out the demon which resided there. The wounds were then rubbed with soot or charcoal or, in later days, gunpowder.

The Mides knew remedies for all sorts of ailments. One "sure cure" for an earache was "bear gall," a substance extracted from a freshly killed animal which was dried, powdered, and dissolved in water, then dropped into the ear. Each Mide carried a Mide sack in which he or she kept sacred objects. Highly valued fetishes were often some abnormality of nature, such as a deformed bird's leg, which endowed its owner with special powers of communication with the manitous.

The Delaware Indians had a similar organization called the Great Snake Society whose members roamed about from band to band curing diseases and presiding over funerals.

Algonkian tribes had other mystery men besides the priests or shamans. These were sorcerers, prophets, and herbalists who worked individually, performing rites, and giving out medicine for a fee. Sorcerers exerted great influence over the Indians with their curative powers and abilities to ward off disasters. These men went through all sorts of wild contortions and called upon the supernatural. They were said to suck the demons from a sick person through a bone tube. Many of these wizards were frauds who deceived not only their tribesmen with their "magic" but themselves as well. One Algonkian sorcerer named Pigarouich lived in the early 1600's and gave an account of some of his activities to a French missionary. He told of the special lodge in which a tribal wizard lived. It was a tent about seven feet high, from which the sorcerer called to the spirits. The tent could be made to shake and sway and loud noises could be heard coming from the inside when the spirits were arriving. Pigarouich claimed that sometimes the tent would bend almost to the ground and the sorcerer ran out from his shaking lodge fearing that the earth had opened under him. Pigarouich was greatly feared by his people but, although he fell back into his old ways several times, the famous sorcerer was eventually converted to Christianity by the missionary.

Knowledge of medicinal plants was very important among all the tribes of the Northeast. The Tuscaroras, sixth nation of the Iroquois, have a legend which tells how they learned of the medicine plants. This story was told by Chief Mt. Pleasant, a member of the Bear Clan of the Tuscarora tribe.

A sickly old man came into an Indian village and stopped at each lodge to ask for food and shelter. He was turned away from the lodges of all but the Bear Clan where he was received by a kind old woman. The ailing man told the woman that in order to make him well she must gather certain plants. Each time one sickness was cured the old man came down with another, and each time the woman went into the forest and gathered the plants as he instructed. Finally, the man was well and he told the woman that he had come to teach her people the secrets of medicine. As she was the only one who was kind to him, a great hemlock tree would grow before her home to show that the Bear Clan's medicine was strongest of all the tribes.

One of the most important Iroquois medicine societies was based on a legend about a hunter who was kind to animals. The story goes that when enemies attacked and killed this hunter the animals of the forest mixed a magic liquid which brought him back to life. To the liquid each animal added a tiny "life spark." The medicine they made was so concentrated that it could easily be contained in an acorn shell and was for this reason known as the Little Water. The organization became known as the Little Water Company. The society conducted night-long ceremonies consisting of songs which told the legend of the good hunter.

Another medicine society of the Iroquois used grotesquely carved masks as part of its ritual. The masks, called false faces, were worn by members of the False Face Society, who went about protecting people from evil spirits and curing diseases.

There are several tales connected with the wearing of the masks. According to some, the faces are likenesses of the mythological Great Heads, bodiless beings of the forest who could be called upon to aid the wearer of the mask. Another story tells that long ago the Stone Giants devoured so many Iroquois people that the Sky Holder had to come to the aid of the unfortunate Indians. He told the people to hide in caves, then shook the land with tremendous force, crushing all but one of the Giants, who escaped with a twisted face. The Giant became the

Members of the False Face Society

master of a race of hideous-faced spirits. A hunter who met the Stone Giant in the forest was told that, to be rid of disease, faces in the spirits' likenesses must be carved from living basswood trees and worn at certain ceremonies.

To become a member of the Society one had only to dream that he was a False Face. He then told the proper person, gave a feast, and was initiated. All members of the organization were male except one who was the Keeper of the False Faces. She alone knew the names of all the members, since they were always masked at ceremonies and never saw each other's real face. When they wore their masks the Society members believed they became the spirit shown by the mask.

Someone who was ill simply notified the Keeper of the False Faces, who then led the masked members to that person's home. They came shaking turtle rattles and, upon arrival, sprinkled ashes on the patient, carried out other rites, and left. It is said that they never failed to cure nosebleeds, toothaches, and eye swellings.

Each fall and spring, members of the False Face Society went about the village conducting a ceremony to frighten away evil spirits. Traditionalists among the Iroquois have continued this practice to this day.

One story tells that the masks were two brothers' heads, one black and one red. They had a cousin whose face was half red and half black. A carver, who roughed out the mask in a living tree, painted it red if he had begun in the morning or black if it was started at night. A black and red mask was a whirlwind mask because it was thought that it could divert storms if hung facing the wind. Masks were made in variations of about twelve main types. These included a crooked-mouth, spoon-lipped, tongue-protruding, and laughing beggar face. Later mask makers added metal rings or discs around the eyes and long horsehair, giving the false faces a very eerie appearance.

Masks made of cornhusks were worn by members of the Huskface Society, who impersonated spirits of the harvest and performed at the Midwinter Ceremony and the Green Corn Festival. Masks of buckskin represented cannibal clowns or "Long Nose," the kidnapper of naughty children.

Mask making has all but disappeared among the modern Iroquois, but the Indians still retain some of their masks and use them at ceremonies. They believe in feeding their false faces and do this by smearing tobacco and sunflower oil on the mouths of the masks. Although many outstanding examples of Iroquois masks are in museums today, the Indians do not like them kept there and feel that the faces are unhappy imprisoned in the glass display cases.

The Algonkian tribes of Delaware and Mohegan Indians used masks also. The Delaware masks were similar to the Iroquois but were worn at a Corn Harvest Dance, an annual festival to Mother Corn. At the Big House Ceremony of the Delaware a masked dancer represented a guardian spirit who controlled sickness and the deer hunt.

The Iroquois were influenced greatly in the late eighteenth and early nineteenth centuries by a prophet who appeared among the Senecas. This religious man was called Ganiodaya, which means "It Is a Very Large Lake." He is more commonly remembered as Handsome Lake and was the half-brother of the famous Chief Cornplanter, once greatly honored by the colonists for his friendship. Handsome Lake's main objective was to improve relations with the white men by adopting some of their ways while still retaining many of the Indian traditions. He had become a heavy drinker of the liquor with which white men were supplying the Indians. It was not until a group of Quakers came among his people preaching the Christian religion that Handsome Lake began to have his visions. In one of these visions Handsome Lake was told to stop drinking and, according to the prophet, he then reformed and went about preaching to his people.

His words became known as the Code of Handsome Lake or the Good Message, and included the story of the prophet's vision and a code listing rules for family life and manners. He described a Heaven, and a Hell in which there was a Devil called the Evil Minded. According to Handsome Lake, Hell was not a permanent place and from there the Indian went to Heaven, which was called the New World, a paradise of berry-picking. In Heaven, families were reunited and lived together forever with a bodily form and memories of their earthly life. This was strictly an Indian Heaven and white men did not go there. Handsome Lake advocated the killing of witches and did not want any Indian children to attend a white man's school. Sosheoa, Handsome Lake's grandson, established an oral text of the Good Message. The religion of this great Iroquois prophet was adopted by many of his people and is yet today a source of guidance and inspiration for many of these tribesmen. The Good Message is recited once a year in the long houses of the Iroquois.

All the Indians of the Northeast entertained their children with fanciful tales and stories explaining natural phenomena. Some Algonkian tribesmen told their children that there was a woman in the moon boiling corn in a kettle. The Iroquois told their youngsters that one of the star clusters was an old man who was tired of his earthly life and had been given a place in the sky to live by the four spirits of the wind. The Chippewa told of a sandman who, in summer, came riding on the back of a firefly. This was the little fellow known as Weenk who brought his warriors to help close the eyes of Chippewa youngsters. Many animal stories, some of which are familiar to white children, are of Indian origin. "How the Bear Lost Its Tail" and "The Great Bear in the Sky" are both Iroquois legends which are known by most Americans.

During long winter nights in the far north the Naskapi Indians told this story of the Deer and the Squirrel to their children. A reindeer called all the mammals and birds together and said that he would give each a name. When he came to the squirrel he asked the bushy-tailed little creature what he would like to be called. The squirrel replied that he wanted the same name as the black bear. The reindeer patiently explained to the small rodent that it was much too tiny to take on the name of so great an animal. The squirrel began to cry and wept so long that its lower eyelids turned white. This is why the squirrel has white fur under its eyes.

The Chippewa sandman

Chapter 9

CULTURAL EXCHANGE

IN THE SHADOWS of a Chippewa lodge the ancient teller of legends recounted a family story.

"A white man gave Iagoo a gun, so my grandfather said. Iagoo learned how to shoot it better than any white man.

"Iagoo paddled his canoe into the wild rice fields and waited for the ducks. A great flock flew up and darkened the sky. Iagoo lay on his back in the canoe and shot straight into the air. A swan fell dead into his canoe and the ducks fell all about him until the water was black with the dead birds. Iagoo piled them up in a high mound on the shore.

"The shot from Iagoo's gun fell back into the lake and hit two loons. It went right through the loons and killed a muskellunge. No one else ever fired such a shot as Iagoo. He told this story to my grandfather."

The gun was but one of many "gifts" with which the Europeans astounded, intrigued, and transformed the Indian, but what the white man received from the natives made possible his very existence in the New World. As a result of the cultural exchange between red man and white, an ancient way of life was lost and a new nation was born.

The white men who first arrived on the North American continent discovered that to survive in this newly found wilderness they must adopt many native practices. Foremost among Indian contributions to their pale-skinned guests were the secrets of procuring food. Algonkians taught the coastal settlers agricultural methods and introduced them to food heretofore unknown to European palates. Maize, beans, squash, and pumpkin were food items which the early colonists learned to grow, prepare, and preserve. From these vegetables the white men made Indian dishes, including succotash, hominy, baked beans, and roasted corn. The natives pointed out the wild deer and the abundance of edible shellfish. They instructed the Europeans in the use of fish as fertilizer for their crops. The eastern Indians taught the settlers that when the seeds of corn and beans were sown together in one hill the plants grew up together, the beans climbing up the cornstalks.

Among the Indians who were of considerable help to the early white men was Squanto. This Indian, known also as Tisquantum, appeared in Plymouth Colony one day in March, 1621, and addressed the astonished Pilgrims in English. This marvelous individual was referred to by the Pilgrims as "a speciall instrument sent of God for their good beyond their expectation." The lingual abilities of Squanto were not heaven-sent but rather acquired from a long stay in English company. Accounts are varied, but it is thought that Squanto had been kidnapped from Patuxet in 1614 by a Captain Hunt who sold him as a slave in Spain. Spanish monks freed the copper-skinned foreigner who then went to live in England and was later brought to Newfoundland. Captain Thomas Dermer took Squanto along the New England coast one year as an interpreter and it was in this way that the former citizen of Patuxet returned to his home, only to find his people had died or moved away and the English settlement of Plymouth was standing on the site of his vanished village. Squanto lived only a short time but was a most valuable

Squanto

aid to the Pilgrims as an interpreter, teacher, and guide. It was Squanto who told the Pilgrims to plant their corn "when oak leaves were the size of a mouse's ear."

Another chief, known as Samoset (He Who Walks Over Much), who knew a smattering of English from contact with local fishermen, was even more helpful, for it was through him that the Pilgrims met Wasamegin, more commonly called Massasoit, the grand sachem of all the Wampanoags. This powerful chief made a treaty with the Pilgrims and remained a loyal friend to the colonists until he died almost fifty years later.

In addition to teaching the early immigrants how to grow food, the Indians had much influence on white hunters who adopted both the dress and hunting techniques of the natives as they pursued the fur-bearing animals of the northern forests. Information about the forest animals was a gift from the Indians which enabled Europeans quickly to familiarize themselves with America's commercial potential and to establish a great fur trade. The early hunters became expert at tanning hides and fashioning deerskin clothing in the manner of the natives. Frenchmen, especially, learned to live with the Indians, tracking and trapping the otter, beaver, muskrat, and deer. In appearance and in ability to hunt the woodland creatures, these men practically became Indians but for one outstanding difference. The white hunter trapped the animals in search of profit, a concept as yet unknown to his dark-skinned tutors.

Fishing methods, too, were learned from the Indians, who showed their white friends how to trap and net fish from the sparkling streams and how to fish through the ice of northern lakes. The hunters and fishermen even adopted the Indian's lean-to shelters as temporary homes in the forest.

Native methods of transportation included canoes and snowshoes. The lightweight birchbark canoes were quickly adopted by the earliest explorers and similar craft are in use today throughout the forests of the Northeast. The modern open Canadian canoe is directly descended from the Indian birchbark. The Pilgrims bought a few birchbark canoes from the Indians, but their unpracticed handling of the tipsy boats had some unpleasant consequences. After a dunking or two most of these colonists acquired the more stable log dugouts. In winter, when ice made the rivers and lakes impassable by canoe, Indian-type snowshoes were worn by the rugged white hunters. Toboggans, copied from the forest people, were used to haul the fresh-killed game, skins, and furs over the winter snow.

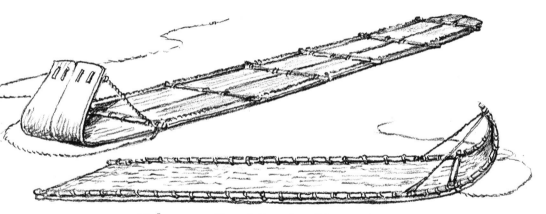

Toboggans: Cree (above) and Iroquois

Few trails needed to be blazed through forests and mountains of the East, for explorers found the land already crisscrossed by thousands of Indian-made paths. These primitive roads were less than eighteen inches wide, yet they had been worn a foot deep into the earth by the tread of numberless skin-clad feet. The Indian trails led conveniently from one stream to another, and the white men learned from the natives to carry their canoes over these portages. Indian trails were noted for their directness and avoidance of obstacles. Trained native runners along these well-worn pathways are said, at times, to have covered up to one hundred miles between sunrise and sunset of a single day. So good were these earliest trails that almost the entire system of roads in the eastern United States today follows the ancient paths of the Indians. The route taken by Daniel Boone into Kentucky was an Indian trail known as Warrior's Path.

This contribution to travel in America was made by the Indians long before Europeans even knew of this land. The conversion of Indian trails to white men's roads was once commented upon by Nathaniel Hawthorne who said, ". . . and the Indians coming from their distant wigwams to view the white man's settlement marvel at the deep track which he makes and perhaps are saddened by a flitting presentiment that this heavy tread will find its way over all the land." Some Indians viewed the white encroachments with deeper feeling. This statement was made in 1847 by Peter Wilson, a Cayuga: "The Empire State, as you love to call it, was once laced by our trails from Albany to Buffalo; trails that we have trod for centuries; trails worn so deep by the feet of the Iroquois that they became your roads of travel, as your possessions gradually ate into those of my people. Your roads still traverse those same lines of communication which bound one part of the Long House to the other."

The Indians provided the interpreters who enabled explorers to travel through much of interior North America. Many of these were children of French men and Indian women.

Many Indian tribes have simply disappeared, either destroyed or assimilated with the passing of time. Lasting testimony to these vanished peoples is to be found throughout North America, for even though they are gone, their words live on in the names of hundreds of counties, towns, cities, rivers, lakes, and mountains. Some of these were named for tribes or their villages. Most Indian place names were descriptive of a locality. They furnished necessary information known by one Indian to another. This information was usually connected with hunting and fishing, giving a food source or the set of a current. Villages which grew up on the site retained the name. Saco, a town in Maine, means "the outlet of the river," and Damariscotta is translated as "the place of abundance of fishes."

State names with eastern Indian origins include Connecticut, Massachusetts, Ohio, Illinois, Michigan, Mississippi, and Wyoming. Ohio is an Iroquois word for "beautiful river" and Mississippi comes from the Algonkian *misi sipi* or "great water." The western state of Wyoming derives its name from M'cheuwomink, the name of a Delaware village in Pennsylvania. It means "Upon the Great Plain." Well-known cities and towns with Indian names include Schenectady ("end of the trail"), Chicago ("skunk place" or "powerful"), Toronto (Huron word for their lands meaning "land of plenty"), Kalamazoo ("boiling pot," from bubbling springs found there by the Indians), Oshkosh (named for a Menominee chief).

Nantucket Island was named from the Indian word meaning "the faraway place." The Adirondack Mountains are named for the Adirondack Indians and the name, meaning "tree eater," was given to these people by their neighbors, since in times of want the Adirondacks made soup from boiled bark. Countless other place names of Indian origin include rivers such as the Monongahela and the Susquehanna, the Canadian province of Ontario, Chesapeake Bay, Niagara Falls, Penobscot Bay, Montauk Point, Manhattan Island, Saginaw Bay, Lakes Huron, Erie, Michigan (from Michigami, meaning "large body of water"), and Ontario. Every state and province in North America has hundreds of such examples which could be added to a list of locations with Indian names.

Other Indian terms were incorporated into the languages of North America. The majority of these words are Algonkian, for it was with these people that the early white man had the most frequent contact. American-English contains many of these and about a hundred Indian words are a part of the French language in Canada.

Naturally, words for foods like succotash, from the Narraganset *misickquatash* meaning "an ear of corn," and hominy, from the Algonkian *rockahominie* or "parched corn," were readily adopted in the absence of a European word corresponding to the new foods. Animal names for the moose, opossum, terrapin, raccoon, and muskellunge likewise became part of the white man's vocabulary. Moose comes from the Massachuset word *moos* meaning "he strips off" or eats the bark of trees. Raccoon is from the Algonkian word *arakunum* meaning "hand scratcher." Words familiar in American political history include powwow, sachem, mugwump, and Tammany. Powwow is from a Massachuset word *pauwaw* meaning "he dreams" and also refers to a medicine man. Mugwump, the name for an independent political figure, comes from the Algonkian word *mugquomp*, translated as "chief" or "big man."

The American use of the word "Tammany" for the Tammany Society and Tammany Hall had its origin with a famous seventeenth-century chief of the Delaware Indians. This chief, whose name was Tamanend, was believed by the Indians to have been favored with special communications with "the Great Spirit." He was one of the signers of the deed of 1683 giving the lands near Philadelphia to William Penn. The virtuous old chief was so admired among both the Indians and his white friends that he was called Saint Tammany. It was after the illustrious Tamanend that the newly organized Tammany Society was named in 1786. Though the Society degenerated in later years, at its founding by veterans of the Revolutionary War it was dedicated to liberty. Its members met in a "wigwam" and called their officers "sachems."

Other loan words from the eastern Indians are hickory, tama-

Frenchman and Indians

rack, papoose, totem, toboggan, mackinaw, moccasin, and toma-hawk. Various expressions commonly used in America are also connected with the Indians. They include Indian Summer, pale-face, medicine man, bury the hatchet, and pipe of peace.

According to many people, and especially noted by the Iro-quois, the very essence of democracy in the United States orig-inated with the Indians. Our system of government, which provides sovereignty of the states, is said to have been modeled after the Iroquois Confederacy in which each tribe was inde-pendent but united in time of need. The six foundations of the League of the Iroquois were health, happiness, righteousness, justice, power, and strength of character. How much the peculiar character of the American Indian changed the course of history or influenced Europeans in becoming Americans can never be known, but democratic government, brotherhood in society, and equality of rights were certainly more characteristic of the Indian society into which the white immigrants stepped than of the European societies from which they came.

One of our national holidays is Indian in origin. Many Indians held an annual Thanksgiving which lasted about two weeks. Our Thanksgiving Day is an imitation of the Indian festival, even to the foods which we serve. Turkey, cranberries, and Indian pudding are all foods borrowed from the red men.

Tobacco, a plant which the Indians believed was given to them by the gods, was used in America long before the days of Columbus' arrival. The leaves smoked by the Algonkians were called *kinnikinnick*, meaning "what is mixed," since the Indians smoked a combination of tobacco and other leaves. The natives smoked the tobacco because they believed it to be medicinal and it was for this property that Europeans began to use it. Less than a hundred years later tobacco was known throughout the world.

Other herbs and medicinal plants were shown to the early explorers and colonists, often of necessity in the saving of their lives. The Frenchman Cartier and his men spent one terrible winter in Quebec where many died from disease. One friendly Indian gave the rest of the miserable men a mixture of pine needles and bark and saved their lives. The men had been suffering from scurvy which was remedied by the Vitamin C in the Indian medicine.

Lacrosse, the favorite sport of the northeastern tribes is now a popular American game. Indian legends are told today as part of the folklore of America, and even the beauty reflected in Indian artwork is a contribution to our heritage.

The Indian contributed a great deal to the white man's society in North America and to some extent his influence was felt in Europe and throughout the world. But the impressions that the North American natives made upon European culture is small in comparison with the white man's effect upon the Indian. The primitive people of the eastern woodlands who relied upon their religion for explanation of events in their world felt the deep impact of the white man's superior society upon their own. Huge ships, thundering weapons, iron tools, colorful clothes, fascinating trinkets, and alcohol—all the luxuries of European living suddenly introduced to a people but little past the Stone Age had disastrous results. No longer were daily events explainable by superstition. The Indian priests and sorcerers were unable to give guidance in the face of so bewildering and marvelous a people. Thousands of new articles and ideas falling upon an ancient way of life disrupted the Indian socially and morally. The Indian culture had always been based upon the men doing the fighting and hunting and the women managing the house and crops. Suddenly there were iron kettles, knives, axes, hoes, and needles. What need had the Indian to spend laborious hours making things from wood, stone, and bone? Traditional craftwork declined and virtually disappeared. Guns replaced the bow and arrow and made the killing of animals a simple task. The Indian male had little left to occupy his time. With guns given to them by traders, the Iroquois practically exterminated the beaver in their land and by 1650 were forcing their way into adjoining territories. When the Indians acquired guns they found that not only was the hunting of game made easier, but also the slaughtering of traditional enemies. Many tribes sought to extend their territories by using the Dutch, French, and English guns. Some historians feel that, had it not been for the guns which the Iroquois got from the early Dutch, these tribes might have eventually been overwhelmed by the more numerous Algonkians who surrounded them. Thus armed, by the dawn of the eighteenth century, less than 20,000 Iroquois had become the rulers of an area from Canada to Tennessee and Maine to Lake Michigan.

The white man gave the natives liquor which had terrible results, for it broke down emotional control, a carefully cultivated part of Indian character. Apparently, the Indians had to become accustomed to the white man's drink, for in 1606 Marc Lescarbot, an historian and frequent visitor to the coastal Indians, wrote this:

"It was showed them, in pressing the grape into a glass, that of which we did make the wine of which we did drink. We would have made them drink of the wine, but having taken it into their mouths, they spit it out, so ignorant is this people of the best thing that God hath given to man, next to bread."

It did not take long for this European contribution to the native culture to become one of the most splendid bartering items of the traders.

Far worse than any of the things which the Europeans handed the Indians outright were the diseases to which the once-isolated native populations had no immunity. Before long, the Indians were dying by the thousands from smallpox, chicken pox, and measles. It was on the site of the Wampanoag village whose people had died of smallpox that the Pilgrims built Plymouth. When the Hurons first became allies of the French, their tribesmen numbered 30,000. French contact brought about epidemics which, by 1640, had reduced their numbers to 12,000. The fur trade changed the Indian's whole way of life. Instead of hunting only for his food and clothing, he now killed for the pelts with which he could trade for European luxuries. Tribal rivalries over hunting territories fomented dissension and wars, while European disagreements encouraged various alliances of Indian with white. The people of the forests, once proud and free, had become slaves of the fur traders.

Seneca medicine man

With the traders, explorers, and colonists came the missionaries and, not content to let the Indian practice his ancient religion, these men of the church endeavored to make converts of all the North American natives. The French Jesuits concentrated on the Algonkians, since it was with these people that their countrymen were friendly. Naturally, most Indian priests and sorcerers were much opposed to efforts by the missionaries for, with each convert they made, a little more of the Indian priest's power slipped away. Tehorenhaegnon, a Huron medicine man who was considered one of the greatest sorcerers of his time, blamed his rain-making failures upon the crosses which stood before some of the Jesuit houses. In addition, he claimed that they were the cause of drought, famine, and fires in his village. Unfortunately for Tehorenhaegnon, his magic potions brought no relief and his people eventually lost faith in his power.

The first Indian to be made a Catholic nun was a Mohawk girl called Tekakwitha. She was so impressed with the Jesuit missionaries who came into her village in 1668 that she converted to Christianity, thereby angering a great many of her tribesmen. Catherine Tekakwitha, who is also known as the Lily of the Mohawks, has had some fifty biographies written about her in ten different languages. There is a cross in memory of "the Indian Saint" at Auriesville, New York, close to the site of the village where Catherine was born.

Many Indians were converted to Christianity and many staunchly defended the Jesuits. The Hurons, who were probably the best friends of these missionaries, had one chief called Taratwane who stood up in a council meeting at which the lives of some Jesuits were being threatened. Taratwane presented the council with a string of wampum and declared, "There is something to close your mouths and stop your talking." The Jesuits have been both heralded and criticized for their work among the Indians, but it remains a fact that their accounts, known as the *Jesuit Relations*, have yielded much historical information about the early Indians.

Not all the Indians were so favorably impressed with the European missionaries. Especially hostile were the Iroquois, who were considered fiends by the Jesuits. In 1805 the famous Seneca chief, Red Jacket, spoke for many of his people when he uttered this reply to a speech by a missionary:

Mohawk in European clothes

"Brother, our seats were once large, and yours were very small; you have now become a great people, and we have scarcely a place left to spread our blankets; you have got our country, but are not satisfied; you want to force your religion upon us."

Yet one Iroquois, called Thayendanegea or Joseph Brant, was a Mohawk who joined the Anglican Church and translated parts of the Bible into the Mohawk language.

The Iroquois began to use silver ornaments when the French and Dutch first introduced them to the shiny new metal. Later, these Indians pounded out and cut ornaments from silver coins and medals which they received as payment for land. By the end of the eighteenth century there was a silversmith in every Iroquois village. European-type crosses and brooches were worn as jewelry. An Indian measured his wealth by the number of silver brooches he wore and some of the more affluent Indians wore several hundred of these on one garment. The native silversmiths also made headbands, earrings, bracelets, and rings. The Indians of the Great Lakes made silver articles engraved with scrolls, loops, hearts, and flowers, in contrast to the Iroquois' more geometric forms. They also made gorgets, half-moon shaped ornaments which were imitations of European military decorations, a vestige of the medieval breastplate.

The introductions of broadcloth, silk, velvet, glass beads, better threads, and metal needles allowed the northeastern Indians to do more complicated pattern work on their clothing and bags. Glass beads made in Venice, Italy, were the first kind given to the Indians by explorers. These beads were large and used as ornaments but not in sewn work. About 1675, smaller beads were imported and Indian beadwork began. The common "seed" bead became the standard form about 1800 and has been used ever since then. The Indian combined the use of European-made beads with two of the white man's pattern ideas—the double curve and the floral design—and created a semirealistic beadwork style that became characteristic of native craftwork in the eastern United States.

The Iroquois did lacy, curving patterns, using white beads sewn onto dark cloth. Their designs were simple until about 1800 when they began to use a coarse floral design on articles which they sold to tourists at Niagara Falls. The raised encrusted form of beadwork was common among the Indians of New England, and the Penobscot and Passamaquoddy Indians continue the craft today.

The style of the Great Lakes Indians in the 1700's was simple, using few curves in preference to zigzag and diamond shapes, done in white beads. By the mid-1800's the floral patterns took hold and were fashioned in many colors. The Ojibwa (Chippewa) still do some of this beadwork with their own variations.

Each time the Indians adopted a new material or idea from the white man a bit of their own culture faded and died. The silver, glass beads, floral design, and modern materials gradually replaced skins, quillwork, moose hair, native dyes, and simple design. Jewelry, bedspreads, tablecloths, blankets, and bags were all made and designed as fashionable articles to suit European tastes. Even Indian moccasins were cuffed with embroidered broadcloth and velvet. Indian clothing was cut and sewn, using red and blue broadcloth, flannel, and calico. At first, the cloth garments retained the traditional Indian style, but later they were patterned after the clothing of the Europeans. Better sewing methods and the use of buttons resulted in the Indian wearing trousers and coats much like the white men.

Other European contributions to Indian society included foods such as peas and watermelons. Livestock—pigs, geese, ducks, and chickens—were imported, and the Indian was even introduced to the common house cat.

Although the Indian accepted the European inventions and ideas which transformed his way of life, he also resented the changes wrought by the white man's culture. As he watched his lands continually slipping away and his people forced from their homes, he turned upon the intruders. Hatred and vengeance, combined with the newly acquired guns, knives, and axes, made the bronzed native a fearful adversary. For more than two centuries the red man battled to regain his country, but it was a futile fight and one in which he was destined to become the loser.

Chapter 10

―――――◆――――

THE WHITE MAN—FRIEND
AND FOE

"AN UNWORTHY SHIPMASTER whose name was Hunt, being sent forth into these coasts on the account of the fishing trade, after he had made his dispatch and was ready to sail, (under pretence of trucking with them) enticed the Indians into his vessel. They in confidence with his honesty went aboard, to the number of twenty from Patuxet, since called Plymouth, and seven from Nauset (now known by the name of Eastham). These did this Hunt seize upon, stowed them under hatches, and carried them to the straits of Gibralter, and there did he sell as many as he could of them for 20 £, a man, until it was known whence they came. Then the friars in those parts took away the rest of them, that so they might nurture them in the Popish Religion. The pernicious and avaricious felony of this shipmaster, in stealing and selling the Indians to the Spaniards as hath been expressed, laid the foundation to great troubles which did after that befall the English, especially in the northeast part of this land."

―from *A Relation Of The Troubles Which Have Happened In New England By Reason Of The Indians There* by Increase Mather

The Indians met with an assortment of Europeans whose attitudes with regard to the native Americans ran from positive dislike to brotherly love. There were the treacherous, the mistrustful, the indifferent, the righteous, and the good. Some tried to exterminate the red man, some tried to ignore him, others tried to live with him, a few tried to convert him, and even fewer tried to understand him.

First came the Vikings, who had brief but unpleasant contacts with the Indians. Many years later the real influx of Europeans began, slowly at first, as the adventurous explorers charted the way. From 1500, fishermen ranged the coastal waters from Newfoundland southward and many of these became friendly with the Indians. Soon Dutch and English trading vessels were common sights for the dusky men and women of the shores at which these ships stopped. Some of the traders bartered in good faith with the natives and their visits were happy occasions for the Indians. Others, looking for added profits, shanghaied unsuspecting natives onto their ships and sold them as slaves in Europe. The infamous Thomas Hunt was responsible for the kidnapping of Squanto from Patuxet.

The Indians, possessors of the land for thousands of years, had naturally located their villages in the most favorable places to be found. These choice spots included the Delaware and Chesapeake Bays, the Delaware, Susquehanna, and Potomac Rivers, New York Harbor, the Hudson and Connecticut Rivers, Massachusetts Bay, and along the east-west corridor through New York State—all the places which the white man thought would make the best areas of settlement for himself. The Europeans proceeded to negotiate for and buy these lands, and the purchases were often made after the Indian owner had been given sufficient liquor to induce a sale. An Indian once made this statement to Sir William Johnson, the English Indian agent, "You English buy territory by use of the bottle." Not all land purchases were made unfairly and, in many cases, the Indians gave lands outright to the white colonists. Soon the Indians realized that the more the white man traveled into their lands the more lands he would desire and the result would be an eventual loss of native territory. For this reason the Indians tried to restrict European travel to a north-south direction along the Atlantic coast in order to prevent whites from moving westward.

Negotiating for land

It has been stated by some that the English were far less tolerant of the natives than were the Dutch and Swedish settlers of the New World. There were, of course, fewer Dutch and Swedish settlements in America but, even so, the Dutch were not always friends to the Indian. The Dutch settlement of New

167

Amsterdam on Manhattan Island was within the territory of the Wappinger Confederacy. By 1643 these Indians had become a nuisance to the Dutch and their Governor is supposed to have authorized the slaughter of a number of these people. He was said to have laughed as one Indian was tortured to death before him. A war with the Wappingers was the result of these actions and it was during this war that a wall was built across lower Manhattan. This wall was the origin of the name of New York City's famous Wall Street.

The Delaware Indians were at peace with the Dutch and Swedish colonists who bought lands from them. When the English Quakers arrived in 1681, the Delawares continued to live in peace with their white neighbors. It was with William Penn that the Delawares, including Tamanend, held their historic treaty meetings. As a result of a 1737 treaty called the "Indian Walk," Penn's son Thomas was not so beloved as his father. An area of land was purchased from the natives with one boundary determined by the distance a man could walk in a day and a half. The Indians said that Penn's men ran instead of walked. "No sit down to smoke, no shoot a squirrel, but lun, lun, lun, all day long," was the complaint made by one of the Indians.

In 1620, that dedicated band of English colonists known as the Pilgrims arrived to begin a new life on lands where the native life had been swept away. The epidemics which had wiped out thousands of Indians were looked upon by the Pilgrims as God's way of ridding the land of "heathens." Yet it was probably through the help of the heathen Wampanoag chieftain, Massasoit, that any of the Pilgrims survived. This Indian came voluntarily into the Plymouth Colony and made a peace treaty in which he generously gave the Englishmen large tracts of his land.

One story told of the illustrious chief, Massasoit, was recorded by the Puritan Governor, John Winthrop. A friend of the Governor named Edward Winslow, who had gone on a trading mission to Connecticut in 1634, had for some reason left his ship and proceeded to travel on foot through the forest to Plymouth. Apparently having lost his way, he called upon his friend Massasoit who offered to guide him home, a two days' journey. Massasoit sent one of his runners ahead to inform the Colony of Winslow's death and to fabricate as many particulars as were needed to convince the colonists of the story. This was done and the Colony was very upset over the whole situation. On the following day, in the midst of the mourning over Winslow, Massasoit appeared with the supposedly deceased traveler. When he was questioned as to why he had sent the false message, Massasoit replied, "That Winslow might be the more welcome, and that you might be the more happy—it is my custom." Massasoit had made the trip to Plymouth specifically to see everyone get a pleasant surprise.

Unfortunately for the colonists, a great many "heathens" remained and, though some were as friendly and helpful as Massasoit, the natives continued to be a deterrent to expansion in New England. A very large tribe known as the Pequots were, at the time of English settlement, the strongest in that area. Under the leadership of a sachem called Pekoath, this tribe had conquered most of the neighboring peoples except for the Narragansets with whom they waged almost perpetual war. Pekoath's successor, Sassacus, shared his view that the English were intruders who interfered with Pequot control. Views differ as to which faction was to blame for the war that resulted. Some say the Pequots murdered a white trader and several other colonists, while other authorities insist that the Massachusetts Bay Puritans, using this old charge for an excuse to do away with their dark-skinned neighbors, massacred the inhabitants of a Pequot village in 1636. Peaceful up until this time, the Pequots then became determined to rid their lands of the English. One Pequot leader named Uncas broke away from the tribe and with his group of followers retook the name, Mohegan. Uncas was a crafty and unscrupulous chief whose name appears in James Fenimore Cooper's novel, *The Last of the Mohicans*, although the real-life Uncas was not the same as the fictional chief nor were the Mohicans the same as Mohegans. Uncas joined with the British, as did the Narragansets who were eager to overpower the Pequots.

Narraganset friendship for the English had been further increased by Roger Williams, who, in 1634, had been banished from Massachusetts for both his religious tolerance and his defense of Indian land rights, and who was sheltered by Canonicus, the Narraganset chief. Canonicus gave to Roger Williams the land upon which Providence, Rhode Island, was founded. Had it not been for this friendship, the Narragansets might well have joined their Pequot enemies just to rid themselves of the English. Canonicus was the same chieftain who, in 1622, had sent to the Governor of Plymouth a bundle of arrows wrapped in a rattlesnake skin—the customary war challenge. The Governor returned the same skin stuffed with gunpowder and bullets. The sachem understood the portent of the message and refused even to touch the snake skin.

As a result of the English-Narraganset-Mohegan alliance, the Pequots were defeated and practically exterminated, with their chief, Sassacus, slain and their tribesmen killed or sold as slaves.

The peaceful relations were to last but a short time, for Canonicus, the Narraganset chieftain, died in 1647 and in about 1662, Massasoit, the earliest and best friend of the Pilgrims passed away. Massasoit had held such influence over his people, the Wampanoags, that while he lived, hardly one unpleasant incident was recorded between these Indians and the English. Regardless of English attitudes or actions, the helpful Massasoit remained their staunch friend and upheld the treaty he had

Massasoit

made with them in 1621. Even the sharpest Indian critics of the time wrote reports praising the old chief.

English settlements grew larger, and more and more the Indian felt the push from land-hungry Europeans. After the death of Massasoit the Plymouth Colony demanded tribute from the Wampanoags and Massasoit's son, Metacom, grudgingly agreed to the English terms.

Metacom, upon whom the English bestowed the name King Philip, privately began preparations for a war in which he hoped to avenge the wrongs done to his people. Secretly he notified other tribes of his impending war. In 1675 the fighting began and the Narraganset sided with King Philip against England. Uncas and his Mohegans remained loyal to the British, in the hope that their native rivals could finally be eliminated. Governor Winthrop sent a messenger to Philip asking why he was warring against England, and the chief replied, "Your governor is but a subject of King Charles of England. I shall not treat with a subject. I shall treat of peace only with the King, my brother. When he comes, I am ready."

The English had underestimated Philip's potential, for at the outset of the war he and his allies were victorious. The Indians had guns and even set up forges in the woods where they did some of their own gunsmithing. Eventually, English military superiority turned the tide and King Philip was defeated. The courageous chief was killed and his severed head was displayed impaled upon a pole. His wife and son, along with other captives, were sold as slaves in the West Indies. Canonchet, a Narraganset who fought with Philip, was sentenced to death for his part in the war. Before his execution he said, "I like it well, for I shall die before my heart is soft, or I have spoken anything unworthy of myself."

The first European settlements north of Maine were French. The French and Indians were partners in the rich fur trade. Unlike the English, Frenchmen cultivated solid friendships with northern tribes, seeking to support rather than to destroy native populations.

It was the early French explorer, Champlain, who unwittingly assisted the English in attaining supremacy in North America. In 1609, in the company of some Algonkin and Huron Indians, Champlain came upon a small group of Mohawks. His native companions informed the explorer that the Mohawks were their ancient enemies and Champlain willingly frightened them away with gunfire. The astonished Mohawks, who had never before encountered firearms, watched two of their party fall before the thunder sticks which had never even touched them. The frightened Indians fled, spreading the tale of the French attack throughout the forests. It was after this small battle, near what was later known as Lake Champlain, that the Iroquois became bitter enemies of the French, an animosity which lasted almost 150 years and a factor contributing to French downfall in America.

Five years after this incident, when the Dutch established a trading post on the Hudson, they found they were on the threshold of Iroquois lands and their closest neighbors were the Mohawks, Keepers of the Eastern Door. Within twenty years the Mohawks and their Iroquois brothers were exchanging the valuable beaver furs for European firearms, and the Dutch had established a very profitable business.

The fur trade brought about new hostilities among the Indian nations competing for European business. The Five Nations and the Hurons (known to the Jesuits as the "good Iroquois") were at odds until 1649 when a very small Iroquois army invaded Huron territory. The Hurons, whose population had been greatly reduced by several epidemics, but which was still greater than that of the Iroquois, fled before the attackers. The Five Nations were triumphant over their ancient enemy and trade rival. Some of the Hurons were adopted, as was the custom, by tribes of the Five Nations. Others joined the Tobacco Nation, the Eries, or the Neutrals, while still others became part of the modern Wyandots. In the same year that they defeated the Hurons, the Iroquois overpowered the Tobacco People. In 1651 they smashed the Neutrals, and a few years later, the Eries.

The Iroquois made a peace of sorts with the French in the 1650's, and it was at this time that some French Jesuits established a mission among them. The peace was of short duration and the French invaded Iroquois lands in 1666.

Jesuit missionary and Iroquois

The League made yet another agreement with the French, and the Five Nations, weakened by so much war, were in no condition to fight any more battles when the Susquehanna at-

tacked them from the south. History might have read very dif-
ferently for the Iroquois had the Susquehanna not lost a great
many people in a sudden epidemic. The Iroquois easily conquered the remaining Susquehanna and by the 1670's were
masters of a vast territory. The Five Nations healed its wounds
and regained its strength, but much of its population was now
comprised of adopted captives. Aware of the power it wielded,
the Iroquois Confederacy became truly unified and it enjoyed
a supreme position both geographically and politically as it carefully played the French against the British. As holders of the
balance of power during the eighteenth century, the Iroquois
prospered, for both countries were overly generous in their hopes
of gaining favor with the League. Remnants of the tribes vanquished by the Iroquois moved about through lands which were
not theirs and many re-established in Canada. The Chippewa
pushed the Fox tribe south where it joined the Sac. The powerful Chippewa also pushed the Sioux farther to the west. Many
Winnebago died from disease or defeat by the Illinois. The Iroquois moved westward into lands belonging to the Pottowatomi,
Miami, and Illinois. The Illinois were later massacred by the
Great Lakes tribes. More Indians became homeless wanderers.

Intertribal politics either clashed or agreed with European
bickerings, but white expansion continued. The Europeans offered bounties for the scalps of the tribes they wished out of the
way. The French paid the Micmacs bounty for Beothuk scalps
and that tribe disappeared from Newfoundland. The Delaware
were repaid for their early generosity to the white man by being
forced from the East and South until their resistance was so low
that they were made subjects of the Iroquois in 1720. These
people became true displaced persons. Some drifted to Indiana
and others to Missouri. Some went to Ontario, where their descendants still live, and a great many ended their wanderings in
Oklahoma. When the Delaware lived in Pennsylvania and New

Jersey they numbered 10,000. A hundred and fifty years later there were but one-sixth that number.

Displaced Indians such as the Delaware moved west into the upper Ohio Valley, which became the subject of dispute between England and France, bringing about the French and Indian War in 1754. The outcome of this war determined which nation was to dominate North America, and England was victorious. Had the Iroquois sided with the French, the story might have been the opposite.

The famous Ottawa chief, Pontiac, is remembered for his part in the French and Indian War. Pontiac, who lived near the Great Lakes, was the organizer of one America's greatest Indian alliances. The Ottawas, who had gotten along well with the French, suddenly found themselves under the thumb of the British in 1760. Pontiac devised a plan whereby the Indian tribes from Lake Ontario to the Mississippi River were joined to end British rule. The chief's idea was to attack all British forts simultaneously in May, 1763, and his conspiracy succeeded well, for in only a few months time eight forts had been captured. Certain that French aid would arrive, Pontiac kept up a five-month seige of Detroit, a fort which he was unable to capture. French help never came, for France had already signed a peace treaty with England and the war was over. The Ottawa chieftain abandoned his dreams of victory and by 1765 was helping the British to restore peace among some of the smaller tribes in the region. Pontiac's aid to the English, against whom the Indians had so recently fought, angered some of his red kinsmen, and in 1769 an Illinois Indian took the life of the great war chief. In 1770 the Illinois were almost wiped out in revenge for this murder.

The Iroquois had refused to take sides during most of the war. One exception to their neutrality was the battle of Lake George, where a number of Iroquois fought for the British. With

Pontiac

the end of French power in North America, the position which the Iroquois had enjoyed for so long also came to an end. No longer could the League play one nation against another, since the only ruler left was England.

Out of the French and Indian War had come one Indian destined to become famous among his people and the whites. The Mohawk youth, Joseph Brant, was only thirteen when he fought in the battle of Lake George. He later became the prodigy of his commander, Sir William Johnson. Johnson had young Brant edu-

Joseph Brant

cated and by 1775 the Indian was a leader within the League and completely dedicated to the British cause in America. It was his influence which brought four of the Six Nations out of neutrality to join the British. Only the Oneidas and the Tuscaroras sided with the Americans. Brant was supposedly so fierce a warrior that he earned the name "the Monster Brant." He was rewarded for his loyalty to the British, who gave him lands along the Grand River in Ontario which later became the Six Nations Reserve. It was here that he made his famous translations of the

English Bible into Mohawk. The Iroquois still loyal to the colonists remained in New York or moved west to Wisconsin.

The Seneca orator, Red Jacket, got this name during the Revolution when he was presented a red coat by the British. Another famous Iroquois, Cornplanter, fought for the British during the Revolution and for the Americans in the War of 1812. He was honored for his friendship toward the Americans, but eventually turned in wrath against all white men.

Following the Revolutionary War, many treaties were signed ceding native lands, often by Indians who had no authority to do so. A series of small wars with the Indians was fought in what was called the Old Northwest (the Indiana, Ohio, Illinois area). It was during one of these wars that the Miami chief, Little Turtle, was defeated. The wars ended with an agreement called the Treaty of Greenville in 1795 which ceded lands to the United States and guaranteed that lands not already given to the whites belonged to the Indian tribes. After the peace, the Americans gave Little Turtle a house and other comforts, hoping in this way to set an example in their efforts to civilize other Indians. But the Indians regarded this as bribery and Little Turtle lost some of his popularity. To regain the respect of his countrymen, Little Turtle often opposed the American authorities but he nevertheless refused ever again to wage war against the United States.

A Shawnee Indian called Tecumseh (Shooting Star) was the leader of the Ohio area Indians after this treaty agreement. He tried to unite his fallen people in a confederacy so that they could live their old way of life. His brother, Tenskwatawa, called The Prophet, preached against the white man's way, denouncing the use of liquor and intermarriage with whites. Tecumseh traveled to many Indian peoples, urging them to organize. He talked to American and British leaders, telling them that the United States had no right to buy lands from individual

Indians when the territory belonged to all the tribes. The Governor of the Northwest Territory, William Henry Harrison, continued to make separate agreements for land transfers. During Tecumseh's absence and against his orders, The Prophet attacked some of Harrison's soldiers. In the Battle of Tippecanoe, which followed, the Indian forces were beaten. Tecumseh returned to a shattered dream and, leaving his homelands, went to Canada. He led troops against the Americans in the War of 1812 and was killed in a battle in which the victorious American troops were led by General Harrison.

The last of the Indian wars in the Old Northwest came about as a result of the treaties signed by the Sac Indian, Keokuk, who was not the legitimate leader of his tribe. Black Hawk, the true head of the Sac, refused to vacate the lands that Keokuk had signed away. Years later Black Hawk wrote in defense of his actions: "My reason teaches me that land cannot be sold. The Great Spirit gave it to his children to live upon. So long as they occupy and cultivate it they have a right to the soil. Nothing can be sold but such things as can be carried away." In 1832, "Black Hawk's War" began and though the Sac and Fox won several small battles, their campaign, too, ended in defeat. Black Hawk died on a reservation ruled by Keokuk, who had been made chief of the Sac by President Andrew Jackson.

After the American Revolution the United States government found that it had to deal with the problem of the Indian if it was to expand its frontiers and meet the needs of a growing population. It began by recognizing the Indian tribes as nations with their own territories. One of the first declarations of Congress made in 1789 embodied this doctrine: "The utmost good faith shall always be observed towards the Indians, their lands and property shall never be taken from them without their consent; and in their property, rights, and liberty, they shall never be invaded or disturbed, unless in just and lawful wars author-

Red Jacket

ized by Congress; but laws founded in justice and humanity shall from time to time be made, for preventing wrongs being done to them, and for preserving peace and friendship with them."

Various administrations of the United States government have made many promises to the Indian which could not be kept, and many times the stated policy was not upheld. Throughout the years laws were passed dealing with the Indian, some of which in their attempt to help him, merely succeeded in taking away more lands and further crushing the spirit of the red man.

Today, many Indians live on the more than three hundred United States reservations. A reservation was originally land upon which the Indians were confined. Now, the term "reservation" means land which is held in federal trust for use by Indians.

181

Indians who live on a reservation are full-fledged United States citizens, free to come and go at will. They pay no taxes upon their lands or on income derived from the lands, and are under federal instead of state jurisdiction. Many have jobs off the reservation and are fully assimilated into the white man's culture. Others find employment in the non-Indian world but return to their reservations periodically.

A few tribes, such as the Penobscots and Passamaquoddies of Maine, live on lands set aside for them by their states. In the case of the Penobscots, families have inherited incomes from funds held in trust for them. The money came from sales of Indian lands to Massachusetts and Maine. These Indians work as guides, boatbuilders, and makers of baskets and bric-a-brac for the souvenir-minded tourists.

Although it has been severely criticized by Indian and white alike, the Bureau of Indian Affairs is the government agency responsible as trustee of Indian lands and for providing public services to the Indians. These services include schools and other aids to education, employment assistance, welfare and health benefits, housing, and development of reservation resources.

Of the eastern Indians, the Iroquois is one large tribe which has retained lands within the boundaries of its ancient territory. Today more than 10,000 of these proud people live in New York State; there are six reservations within New York set aside for them, but a larger segment of the Iroquois population lives in Canada. Many Oneidas who sold their lands in New York now live in Wisconsin. In both the United States and Canada some of the Iroquois people continue in their old traditions by practicing their own religion and preserving the Long House Confederation. The Mohawks have gained fame as the sure-footed construction workers who help build skyscrapers and bridges in cities like New York and San Francisco.

The Chippewa who had once prospered in the fur trade were

deprived of their main source of income when, by 1840, beaver pelts were no longer in demand. Like most tribes, the Chippewa lost their lands and were put on reservations. They, too, were fortunate enough to be located within their ancient homelands, but the Chippewa, largest of the eastern tribes, is also one of the

A modern Indian

183

poorest. Descendants of other Great Lakes Indians live on reservations scattered throughout Michigan, Wisconsin, Minnesota, Iowa, and Canada. Others were moved to Kansas or into Indian Territory, which became the state of Oklahoma in 1907.

Few descendants and little of their artifacts are left to remind us of the once large coastal tribes. Those first Algonkians to greet the white man and the first to shed their blood in defense of their lands are all but vanished.

The tribes which remain are not fading out but are, in fact, increasing their numbers at a rate faster than the rest of the United States population. But the majority of these are poorly housed, poorly clothed, and poorly fed. A great many have no desire to become a part of the white man's culture and they live in fear that even their reservations will some day be encroached upon and taken away.

How inglorious a state for these peoples of ancient lineage, for tribes once so proud and strong and self-sufficient. Those who took from the Indian his forests and streams, built roads over his shadowy pathways, erected cities in the ashes of his villages and over the bones of his fathers—looking back upon recent history, some are touched by the words of the famous orator, Logan, who, in declaiming his own deplorable fate, spoke prophetically for those of his race yet unborn. Logan, whose entire family was murdered in 1774 by a party of nearly thirty misguided white men, is remembered for this short speech, one of the most poignant addresses ever made by an Indian.

"I appeal to any white man to say if he ever entered Logan's cabin hungry, and he gave him not meat; if he ever came cold and naked, and he clothed him not. During the course of the last long and bloody war, Logan remained idle in his cabin, an advocate for peace. Such was my love for the whites, that my countrymen pointed as they passed, and said, 'Logan is the friend of the white men.' I had even thought to have lived with you, but for the injuries of one man. Colonel Cresap, the last spring, in cold blood, and unprovoked, murdered all the relations of Logan, not sparing even my women and children. There runs not a drop of my blood in the veins of any living creature. This called on me for revenge. I have sought it; I have killed many; I have fully glutted my vengeance. For my country, I rejoice at the beams of peace. But do not harbor a thought that mine is the joy of fear. Logan never felt fear. He will not turn on his heel to save his life. Who is there to mourn for Logan? Not one."

Museums with
Woodland Indian Collections

American Museum of Natural History, New York City, New York
Brooklyn Museum, Brooklyn, New York
Buffalo Historical Society, Buffalo, New York
Chicago Natural History Museum, Chicago, Illinois
City of Milwaukee Museum, Milwaukee, Wisconsin
Cleveland Museum of Natural History, Cleveland, Ohio
Cranbrook Institute of Science, Bloomfield Hills, Michigan
Harvard University, Peabody Museum of Archaeology and Ethnology, Cambridge, Massachusetts
Hudson's Bay Company's Museum, Winnipeg, Manitoba, Canada
Minnesota Historical Society, St. Paul, Minnesota
Museum of the American Indian, Heye Foundation, New York City, New York
National Museum of Canada, Ottawa, Ontario, Canada
Newark Museum, Newark, New Jersey
New Brunswick Museum, Saint John, New Brunswick, Canada
New York State Museum, Albany, New York
Rochester Museum of Arts and Sciences, Rochester, New York
Smithsonian Institution, Washington, D.C.
University of Michigan, Museum of Anthropology, Ann Arbor, Michigan
University of Pennsylvania, University Museum, Philadelphia, Pennsylvania
University of Wisconsin, State Historical Society Museum, Madison, Wisconsin
Wayne State University, Museum of Anthropology, Detroit, Michigan

Selected Reading

General Information

American Heritage Publishing Company. *The American Heritage Book of Indians*. New York: Simon and Schuster, 1961.

Bureau of American Ethnology. Reports and bulletins.

Bureau of American Ethnology. *Handbook of American Indians North of Mexico*. Washington, D.C.: Government Printing Office, two vols. (out of print). Reprinted by Pageant Books, Inc., New York, 1959.

Grant, Bruce, *American Indians Yesterday and Today*. New York: E. P. Dutton and Co. Inc., Revised edition, 1960.

La Farge, Oliver. *A Pictorial History of the American Indian*. New York: Crown Publishers, 1956.

National Geographic Society. *Indians of the Americas*. Washington, D.C. Revised edition, 1966.

Tunis, Edwin. *Indians*. Cleveland and New York: The World Publishing Company, 1959.

Woodland Indians

Speck, Frank Gouldsmith. *The Iroquois*. Bloomfield Hills, Michigan: Cranbrook Press, 1945.

U.S. Government Printing Office. *Indians of the Eastern Seaboard*. Washington, D.C., 1967.

U.S. Government Printing Office. *Indians of the Great Lakes*. Washington, D.C., 1966.

Biography

Bonnell Publishing Company. *Biographies and Legends of the New England Indians*. Wakefield, Mass., 1968.

U.S. Government Printing Office. *Famous Indians: A Collection of Short Biographies*. Washington, D.C.

Thatcher, B. B. *Indian Biography*. Two vols. New York and Akron, Ohio: D. M. MacLellan Book Company, 1910.

SELECTED READING

LEGENDS AND MYTHOLOGY

Burland, Cottie. *North American Indian Mythology*. London: Paul Hamlyn Limited, 1965.

INDIAN CRAFTS

Hunt, Ben W. *The Golden Book of Indian Crafts and Lore*. New York: Golden Press, 1954.

Lyford, Carrie A. *Iroquois Crafts*. Lawrence, Kansas: Haskell Institute, 1945.

Lyford, Carrie A. *Ojibway Crafts*. Lawrence, Kansas: Haskell Institute.

Salomon, Julian Harris. *The Book of Indian Crafts and Lore*. New York: Harper and Brothers, 1928.

INDIANS TODAY

U.S. Government Printing Office. *Answers to Your Questions About American Indians*. Washington, D.C., 1968.

U.S. Government Printing Office. *American Indians and the Federal Government*. Washington, D.C., 1966.

Index